"Tony Perkins offers strong, respectable role models for young Christians to emulate as they enter into the world of adulthood. In his book *No Fear,* using a biblical foundation, Perkins tells the stories of young individuals who stand strong in their faith and convictions, despite facing adversity. As the world continues to spiral into an anti-Christian age, it's important to empower our young people with the strength and conviction to hold fast to the teachings of Christ, and *No Fear* does just that."

—DR. JACK GRAHAM, senior pastor of Prestonwood Baptist Church

NOFEAR

TONY PERKINS

INOFEAR

REAL STORIES
OF A COURAGEOUS
NEW GENERATION
STANDING FOR TRUTH

WATERBROOK
PRESS

No Fear
Published by WaterBrook Press
12265 Oracle Boulevard, Suite 200
Colorado Springs, Colorado 80921

Hardcover ISBN 978-1-60142-741-0
eBook ISBN 978-1-60142-743-4

Published in the United States by WaterBrook Multnomah, an imprint of the Crown Publishing Group, a division of Penguin Random House LLC, New York.

WATERBROOK and its deer colophon are registered trademarks of Penguin Random House LLC.

Library of Congress Cataloging-in-Publication Data
Perkins, Tony.
  No fear : real stories of a courageous new generation standing for truth / Tony Perkins. — First edition.
      pages cm
    ISBN 978-1-60142-741-0 — ISBN 978-1-60142-743-4 (electronic) 1. Courage—Religious aspects—Christianity. 2. Fear—Religious aspects—Christianity.
3. Witness bearing (Christianity) 4. Christian biography. I. Title.
    BV4647.C75P47 2015
    243—dc23

                                    2015008739

Printed in the United States of America
2016

10 9 8 7 6 5 4 3

SPECIAL SALES
Most WaterBrook Multnomah books are available at special quantity discounts when purchased in bulk by corporations, organizations, and special-interest groups. Custom imprinting or excerpting can also be done to fit special needs. For information, please e-mail SpecialMarkets@WaterBrookMultnomah.com or call 1-800-603-7051.

Like arrows in the hand of a warrior,
So are the children of one's youth.
—Psalm 127:4

To my quiver of arrows, Kendal, Rachel,
David, Grace, and Samuel: may the Lord use
you to pierce the darkness of your generation.

I love you!
Dad

Contents

Preface

When my first child was born—Anthony Richard Perkins—I had no idea what it meant to be a father. My own father was killed in a railroad accident when I was just three years old, and while I had men I looked up to, I never had a father figure. My mother did her very best as a single mom, and I am grateful that she devoted her life to raising me and my older siblings. She had several opportunities for courtship, but she said protecting and raising me was her top priority. I never knew the full meaning of that until years later.

My wife and I were married at a little church in Cincinnati that she had attended while growing up. I attended with her a few times after we were married, but I didn't care much for the preacher because he seemed to yell a lot. So we quit attending. God was not a part of our lives or our home at the time, but thanks to our son Tony, that would soon change.

The summer before Tony was to start kindergarten, a new church in our town, Grace Bible Presbyterian Church, held a parade through our neighborhood, signing up kids for Vacation Bible School. We thought the interaction with other kids would be a great way to get him prepared for school, so we signed him up. Tony loved Vacation Bible School so much that for weeks afterward he would ask, "Dad, when are you going to take me to Sunday school?" I would always say, "Next Sunday." That went on for several months, until one Sunday I finally gave in.

A five-year-old boy who had never gone to church didn't real-ize that no one sits in the front row. In fact, no one sat in the first five rows that morning except Tony and me, only because I was unable to catch him as he scooted down the center aisle. The Sunday school superintendent looked down at us and said, "Looks like we have some visitors with us this morning." As an introvert, I hated being embarrassed like that. To this day I be-lieve God stuck me to the seat or I would have gotten up and left.

After we had attended for a few weeks, the pastor, Albert Cook, paid us a visit. I must have had a neon sign on my forehead saying I was spiritually lost because he immediately asked me if I was a Christian. When I told him I wasn't, he asked me if I wanted to become one. I wasn't sure what that was all about, but I knew I needed help to be a good father. I always wanted to have a great family and realized I couldn't do it on my own. From that day forward Jesus Christ has been in my heart, and in my wife's heart, and we have done our best to make Him the center of our home.

God used a five-year-old boy to lead me down the right path and has continued to have His hand on Tony ever since.

When Tony was in the fifth grade, he came home one day and said his teacher had told the class we all came from monkeys.

"But God created us," he exclaimed to me.

I told him that was true but not everyone believes it, and then I said something that could have changed the trajectory of Tony's life.

"Just go along with the teacher."

A few weeks later I received a note from the teacher request-ing a conference with me. When I went to the school, Tony's teacher told me he thought Tony had a psychological problem. He explained that he wanted to observe him for a few more weeks, consult with other teachers, and get back to us. I wasn't sure what to expect when we got another note requesting that both my wife and I attend a special meeting with the teacher and the principal.

We went to the school and waited alone in the principal's office before an older female teacher came in with tears streaming down her cheeks.

"Mr. and Mrs. Perkins, there's nothing wrong with Tony," she blurted out. "It's the teacher."

Then the principal came in and apologized for what we had been through.

We later learned that each time the teacher said that humans evolved from monkeys, Tony would stand up and say that it wasn't true, adding, "God created me; I did not come from a monkey."

At the end of the school year, the teacher was fired.

Over the years I've watched Tony repeatedly take a stand for his faith, often facing criticism. For example, after leaving the Marine Corps, Tony was offered a position with a company that provided anti-terrorist training for military and police personnel from over fifty different countries. Tony enjoyed the interaction with the students from so many cultures and would often invite them to his home and join them for weekend activities. When Tony learned there were no Gideon Bibles in the dormitories where the trainees stayed, he bought Bibles for the students in their native languages. Many of the trainees came from former Eastern-bloc nations and had never seen a Bible.

While the students were overjoyed, the bureaucrats in Washington were not very happy when they heard the students were being given Bibles. Despite threats, Tony continued to make the

Bibles available to the students until the company's contract was canceled for reasons that were determined to be false—the company later was awarded a settlement.

Then there was the time when Operation Rescue came to Baton Rouge and Tony videotaped their peaceful demonstrations. Though he was a reserve police officer, he did this as a private citizen. I tagged along and was shocked at the abuse experienced by the pro-life protestors. Tony made the footage available to a local television station, which aired the explosive clips. Additionally, Tony wrote an Op-Ed in a pro-life publication about the alarming scenes at the clinic, which eventually led to successful civil suits for police brutality.

Tony's police chief suspended him for his actions, then later tried to reinstate him when he realized Tony acted within his rights as a private citizen. But Tony declined and accepted an offer from the television station to work as a reporter.

I can't tell you how many times I've watched and just shaken my head as Tony has gone toe to toe with mayors, governors, and even presidents. At first I was concerned for him and how he would survive, then I got to the point I just wanted to warn *them* what they were up against!

I can't think of anyone better suited to tell the stories of those who have no fear of man, only a reverence for God. Tony can spot those whose hearts are gripped by such a love for God that all fear is cast out because that's how he lives *his* life.

I hope this book encourages you to live *your* life completely sold out to God with absolutely no fear of man.

—Richard E. Perkins,
father of the author

NOFEAR

But I will show you whom you should fear: Fear Him who, after He has killed, has power to cast into hell; yes, I say to you, fear Him!

LUKE 12:5

No Fear?

What are you afraid of?

We all have our fears, right? The dark. Snakes. Sharks. Monsters. Things that go bump in the night. The kinds of fears that Hollywood has made a fortune exploiting. Those are the fun fears, the ones we like to talk about or weave into campfire storytelling. What about another kind? A deeper fear that grips you in its icy hands, preventing you from doing the right thing. You know what to do, but you're afraid, mostly about what others will think of you.

Remember Peter? An intrepid follower of Jesus, until it really mattered, until it might get him killed. "I do not know the Man!" he said of his friend and Savior.

What are you afraid of?

I stumbled upon the topic of fear in my personal Bible study a few years ago, and what I discovered absolutely fascinated me! Repeatedly throughout Scripture, whenever God was up to something big—on the eve of a great, history-changing event—He spoke a clear, concise command to ordinary people who were about to do extraordinary things through Him.

"Fear not!"

With few exceptions, when God presented a great opportunity or mission to a particular individual, the assignment came with those two powerful words. "Fear not," He said to

- Abraham when He called him out of Ur to pioneer a new nation (Genesis 15:1)
- Moses, who was to bring God's people out of bondage (Numbers 21:34)
- Joshua, the one who was to lead the people into the promised land (Joshua 1:9)
- Mary, who would give birth to the hope of mankind (Luke 1:30)
- Simon Peter, who would become the apostle of hope (Luke 5:10)
- Paul, who was to be the instrument through which most of the New Testament books were written (Acts 27:24)

This strong admonition to courage was reserved not only for individuals but for entire groups of people as well, like the children of Israel when God set the land of promise before them (Deuteronomy 1:21), or the disciples when Jesus sent them out for the first time to spread the good news (Matthew 10:28). History-changing manifestations of God's power and promise were preceded by a command to overcome the fear that greets those who stand at the threshold of such monumental opportunities.

One of the things that jumped out at me as I studied the "fear nots" of the Bible is that I had never really empathized with the fears of these biblical heroes. I assumed that they obeyed God without any thought of the consequences of their obedience.

Why? Because I knew the end of their stories. They all succeeded! There's nothing like success to make us forget the fear they had to overcome—fear of failure, fear of rejection, even fear of death. We know the outcome, but they didn't. They were ordinary people subject to the same fears you and I would have if we were in their shoes.

Imagine Moses, outnumbered by an enemy king's army, yet God told him to fight them anyway. How would you feel if you faced what appeared to be certain defeat? You'd be afraid, just as he was, but God said, "Fear not."

> Faith says, "I can do all things." Fear says, "What will they think of us? What will they *do* to us?"

This command from the Lord is a common thread woven throughout the pages of Scripture. An old Bible teacher once said that when something is repeated a lot in the Bible, you need to ask yourself, "What's it there for?" So why the focus on fear? Why not "Be careful" or "Be nice to everyone"? What is it about fear that would cause God to bring it up so much? Because He wants us to be faithful and knows that fear cancels out our faith.

Think about it. Faith says, "I can do all things." Fear says, "What will they think of us? What will they *do* to us?"

Faith says, "If God commands it, I'll do it." Fear says, "Maybe He didn't mean that literally."

Faith and fear are opposites—it is impossible for faith and fear to equally coexist in your life. You can't step out in faith if you are shrinking back in fear!

Take for instance Joshua, Moses's assistant, whom modern military leaders have studied because of his military prowess. Moses, the one whom God called from the backside of the desert to lead His people out of bondage, was not allowed to enter the Promised Land because of disobedience. A new generation had come to maturity in the wilderness as the faithless and rebellious generation had died off. It was a history-changing time: time to enter the land of promise and see the formation of a new nation that would forever change human history.

In preparation for this epic event, God promoted Joshua to lead the children of Israel across the Jordan into the land promised to generation after generation over the previous 470 years. As He had done in the past and continues to do today, God preceded His call to action with another order: "Be strong and of good courage; do not be afraid, nor be dismayed, for the LORD your God is with you wherever you go" (Joshua 1:9).

Even though God promised to be with him, Joshua had plenty of reasons to be afraid. The promise to enter the "land of milk and honey" had been passed down from generation to generation with hope and anticipation. It was a promise that no doubt many had held on to in those dark days of bondage in Egypt. But that same promise had been true forty years earlier when the children of Israel refused to cross over into the promised land, choosing instead to believe the report of the ten faithless spies who feared the supersized enemy. Their fear canceled out their faith in God. As a result, the unfaithful spies died almost immediately, and the rest of their generation, with the exception of Joshua and Caleb, spent the next forty years withering away in the wilderness.

Those same giants still inhabited the fortified cities on the other side of the Jordan, giving Joshua plenty to fear, if he chose to. Instead, he chose to listen to God, not his fears.

The only way to counter the fear of man is with faith in God, which provides the courage and the strength that God requires for His world-changing work. That doesn't mean we're never afraid. Only a crazy man swims against the current of his day without a sense of his humanity and the limitations that come with it. Having faith in God means you overrule your fear with a greater fear of disappointing the One who created you and called you to be a world changer.

As a marine squad leader, a policeman, and an elected political leader, I have known fear—even the fear of physical violence. But maybe even a greater fear is the fear of the unknown, and greater than that, the fear of ridicule or rejection from others. Fear is real, but so must be our faith. Roman philosopher and statesman Marcus Tullius Cicero said, "A man of courage is also full of faith."

> The only way to counter the fear of man is with faith in God.

Fear wasn't limited to the Old Testament. The early Christians faced intense spiritual and physical opposition. For example, the disciples were strictly warned to stop their preaching in the name of Jesus. The Jewish leaders threatened them with severe punishment if they did not immediately stop what they were doing, and the disciples had a pretty good idea what might be at stake if they didn't back down. Just weeks prior the authorities had organized a kangaroo court that led to the execution of their beloved Lord.

After they were released from prison on this occasion, you would think "common sense" would prevail. Get as far away from that place as possible. Don't rock the boat. Instead, the Bible says the disciples gathered together in that same city to pray. Not for deliverance or the defeat of their oppressors, but for *boldness* so that they could go right back to proclaiming the word of the Lord, whatever the cost. They faced their fears with their faith, and as a result they "turned the world upside down" (Acts 17:6).

And so can you.

The disciples demonstrated the key to conquering the fears that hold us back and rob us of our potential to be salt and light in a decaying and dark world. Despite the threats, despite the hatred, despite the rejection, they decided to obey God rather than man. In other words, they chose to be empowered by a reverent fear of God rather than to be paralyzed by a cowardly fear of what others might think, say, or do in response to their following God.

Today, I see a swelling wave of younger people choosing to do the same thing. In the pages that follow I will share their stories of courageous obedience to God and look at other biblical characters who stood strong in their faith. I am so encouraged by this new generation of followers of Jesus who aren't backing down from the hostility and vitriol they face for standing firm in their faith. If God is about to once again change the course of history through those who fear Him rather than man, I am convinced He will use these brave new disciples and anyone else who will stand firm in their faith.

What are you afraid of ?

2

A Heartbeat of Courage

The afternoon was beautiful. Sunny. It was not yet officially spring, but in Santa Monica, almost every day feels like it.

The palm tree–lined promenade wasn't nearly as busy during the week as it was on the weekends. The farmers market always drew big crowds on Saturdays and Sundays. Still, during the week there were plenty of shoppers strolling through the variety of specialty boutiques. Others were conducting business or engaging in casual conversations, as they sipped on mochas and lattes at outside cafés that dotted the sidewalks.

A few children raced out of an old-fashioned candy store that sold licorice pipes and candy necklaces, favorites from a more innocent time.

But the warmth of the March sun didn't quite take away the chill as Lila made her way to her destination on 3rd Street Promenade. As Lila walked down the sidewalk in her old jeans and flip-flops, her shoulder-length brown hair was pulled back in a short ponytail. Lila wore an oversized T-shirt, designed to conceal her age and her waistline. It was not the temperature or the steady breeze fluttering in from the Pacific Ocean that prompted the occasional shiver; it was one of those deep, anxious shudders that comes from the anticipation of danger that lay just ahead.

The eighteen-year-old was about to stare down the abortion giant Planned Parenthood for the first time. Face to face. After stepping into a building's atrium, she pressed the button on the elevator, taking her to the second floor at 1316 3rd Street. Paying little attention to anyone standing close by, she continued rehearsing her story: *I'm fifteen years old and I am pregnant by my boyfriend who is twenty-three years old, and I need help.*

The tale had been crafted carefully because such a scenario was not only a lie; it was a felony under California law. Regardless of the circumstances, a fifteen-year-old having sexual relations with a twenty-three-year-old is considered statutory rape. Under California law, as in most states, facilities like Planned Parenthood are required to report suspected cases to law enforcement authorities, something Planned Parenthood is notorious for *not* doing. Why? It would get in the way of their chief aim: conducting an abortion.

The recording device hidden under Lila's T-shirt picked up the sound of her racing heart as thoughts and fears of the "what ifs" flooded her mind.

What if they discover I'm really eighteen and not the fifteen-year-old I am claiming to be?

What could happen to me behind the doors of this clinic if they catch on to our undercover operation?

The thoughts were coming almost as fast as her heart was racing.

"Lord, give me the courage to overcome my fears," she whispered out loud as she walked toward the clinic's busy lobby.

This was the first time Lila had stepped into an abortion clinic, but it was not her first step of courage in a journey that is changing the way America views Planned Parenthood and the abortion industry.

Life as a child was normal for Lila, as normal as growing up with eight siblings can be. Born on July 27, 1988, in San Jose, California, she was the third of eight children born to John and Annie Rose. Lila's parents placed a priority upon both the spiritual and academic development of their children, choosing to educate their children at home and exposing them to the classical teachings of the ancient scholars and church fathers.

But it was not all textbooks and lessons. As with most homeschooled families, activities in the Rose household revolved around

Lord, give me the courage to overcome my fears.

faith and family. Although they were active in their church, the greatest lessons of faith that shaped young Lila were not just taught on Sunday morning but were caught at home as she watched her parents.

Similar to the mostly bygone practice of apprenticeship, children at home learn their moral and spiritual priorities by observing their parents in a variety of settings. Two of those virtues Lila learned at home were a genuine respect for life and the practice of self-sacrifice.

Throughout Lila's adolescent years her parents provided awareness and exposure to the myriad issues confronting her world: homelessness, disease, hunger. The family was involved in building homes in Mexico as well as helping inner-city kids in the Bay Area. Lila took on her own project at sixteen, raising thirty-five thousand dollars for food shipments for famine victims in

Niger. But the fundamental issue of the right to life rose above all others for Lila.

One afternoon in 1997, while at home perusing various books in the family's library, Lila picked up *Handbook on Abortion* by Dr. Jack and Barbara Willke. As she flipped through the pages she came to a creased page. She unfolded it and saw an image that would have a profound and lasting impact on her. For the first time she saw a picture of an aborted baby, and it set the course for Lila's future passion and activism.

"How could anybody do this to a baby?" Lila whispered. As the question remained unanswered, the conviction to do something on behalf of the unborn children swelled. Writing in her journal a few years later at the age of thirteen she penned the words, "It's time to do something about abortion!"

That something came two years later when Lila launched the first Live Action group for teens throughout the Bay Area to bring attention to abortion and promote a culture of life. Lila began giving PowerPoint presentations wherever she found an opportunity, which was primarily before church youth groups. Little did she or anyone else realize that within ten years, Live Action's resources would be on hundreds of high school and college campuses across America. Thousands of students engaged in the cause of life, striking fear in the boardroom of the nation's largest and most aggressive abortion provider: Planned Parenthood.

Her passion grew. When it came time for college, Lila didn't seek a safe harbor for her outspoken views. Instead, she looked for a place where her deep convictions could expose the troubled waters stirred by the fabrications of the radical lost.

Her choice? The University of California, Los Angeles (UCLA).

Lila's choice for an academic major was history, but her focus was pro-life activism. As a freshman in the fall of 2006, Lila expanded her activities to include writing for a pro-life magazine, the *Advocate,* published by the new UCLA chapter of Live Action that she had started upon her arrival at UCLA.

The new publication was designed to bring the truth about abortion and the pro-life movement to the attention of students and faculty. Of course a magazine that advocates for life needed stories that would educate and expose. The *Advocate* marked the beginning of the investigative reporting that would become the hallmark of Lila and Live Action.

Despite the ideologically liberal climate at UCLA, Lila was far from alone on the campus. On almost every university campus, there are students who hold to a core set of traditional moral and cultural values. Many are just afraid to speak up. Soon Lila met an ally in James O'Keefe III, who would later make a name for himself

Many are just afraid to speak up.

when in September 2009 he exposed the corrupt practices of another government-funded organization with ties to President Barack Obama: ACORN.

Rose and O'Keefe's relationship was cemented by the shared experience of being trained in various aspects of activism. Lila received training at the Leadership Institute where O'Keefe was on staff at the time. Just outside Washington, DC, the Leadership Institute focuses heavily on reaching youth with the skills needed to succeed in the rough-and-tumble world of politics and culture.

Back on campus, Lila noticed something odd. In the midst of this "hook-up" culture where promiscuity was the norm, there were no pregnant students. Although birth control was easier to obtain than a vending machine candy bar, you would still expect to see a pregnant student here or there. Why is someone always getting pregnant on popular TV shows like *Glee, Parenthood,* and *The Secret Life of the American Teenager,* but not at UCLA? she wondered. Were the policies and procedures of UCLA officials biased against pregnant students? Did campus officials promote abortion?

There was a story here, somewhere. A story waiting to be told. Lila was sure of it.

That plot came in part through the work of another longtime pro-life activist, Mark Crutcher. In 2002, Crutcher, the founder and president of Life Dynamics Inc., had a young woman, posing as a thirteen-year-old impregnated by a twenty-two-year-old man, call Planned Parenthood clinics seeking advice. The calls, which were recorded, repeatedly exposed clinic workers' recommendation to lie about the circumstances, giving the "thirteen-year-old" assurances that the clinic staff would ignore the mandatory reporting requirements. The recorded evidence was irrefutable.

Rose and O'Keefe were now set; the only difference would be that they would conduct business with the purveyors of abortion not over the phone but in person.

In the fall of 2006, using a hidden recording device, Lila embarked on her first undercover investigation. The target? UCLA's Arthur Ashe Student Health and Wellness Center.

The recorded statements of UCLA's head nurse, Ann Brooks, provided not only answers to the questions; it provided great copy for the inaugural issue of the *Advocate.* The story and the transcript of Brooks encouraging an abortion with advice on how to get "it" taken care of through Rose's parents' insurance without them finding out generated a lot of discussion on campus.

That first undercover operation was a success, and it set the stage for the next investigation that was both bigger and bolder and would thrust Live Action onto the national scene.

Lila stepped off the elevator on the second floor and walked to the entrance of the Planned Parenthood clinic, a blue metal door surrounded by a transom and side windows of opaque glass. The exterior of the clinic looked benign, an almost industrial look that gave no hint of what actually happened inside.

She pressed the intercom button on the protruding chrome box fixed to the wall next to the door.

A very matter-of-fact voice came through the intercom. "Can I help you?"

Using her rehearsed line, Lila bent over toward the chrome box and said, "I am pregnant and I am only fifteen; can I talk with someone?"

There was a buzz, a click, and entrance to the abortion clinic was granted.

Stepping inside, Lila was greeted by the expressionless faces of about a half-dozen women sitting in the small reception area that matched the stolid exterior of the

There was a story here, somewhere. A story waiting to be told.

clinic. She scanned the room, her eyes focusing on the wall behind the young women waiting. The word *Esperanza* was painted there in large letters. Spanish for "hope." It was clear from the downcast faces of the women waiting for their turn that hope was in short supply.

"What's your name?" asked the thirtysomething gatekeeper

dressed in medical scrubs sitting behind the receptionist's counter.

Lila once again recited the statement that she had rehearsed dozens of times in her head. "I am fifteen years old and I think I am pregnant."

The Planned Parenthood staffer ushered Lila behind the reception counter to put some distance between her and others in the waiting room. Behind the counter Lila repeated her situation, adding that her boyfriend was twenty-three years old. In a hushed tone the receptionist said, "If you're fifteen, we have to report it. If you're not, if you're older than that, then we don't need to."

Lila responded, "Okay, but if I just say I'm not fifteen, then it's different? So I could just say . . ."

"You could say sixteen," the woman suggested.

"I could say sixteen?"

"Yes."

"Okay, yeah. So I would just write sixteen?"

"Well, just figure out a birth date that works." With a shrug, the receptionist added, "And I don't know anything."

Lila took the papers and sat down as if she were following the instructions. As other young girls, one by one, stood before the same counter answering questions, others were taken through another door into the back of the clinic where the examinations and abortions were performed. In the midst of the steady flow of activity, Lila slipped out of the door unnoticed with the recorded evidence that Planned Parenthood was aiding and abetting criminal activity.

Because of her bravery, the *Advocate* now had hard evidence of illegal activity. And within days the video they posted on You-

Tube went viral and the story became national news. Lila was interviewed by Fox News's Bill O'Reilly and other news outlets.

In full damage-control mode, Planned Parenthood resorted to legal intimidation of Lila, sending her a cease-and-desist letter. The document stated that her undercover recordings violated California law. They threatened to sue her in civil court for five thousand dollars for each offense. Planned Parenthood demanded she stop the undercover investigations, remove the existing video from YouTube, and turn the original recordings and all copies over to Planned Parenthood.

Lila refused to yield to fear, no matter how strong the attacks against her.

The threat from the billion-dollar abortion giant was more than real to this young woman with only two hundred dollars in her bank account; it was overwhelming. But Lila refused to yield to fear, no matter how strong the attacks against her.

After obtaining legal counsel from the organization Alliance Defending Freedom, Lila reluctantly accepted their advice to comply with some of Planned Parenthood's demands.

However, her undercover work against the organization continues. She has conducted numerous undercover operations exposing Planned Parenthood for rapists and sexual traffickers and for performing illegal late-term abortions. Her courageous work has made her a national leader in the pro-life community and has prompted state and federal investigations into Planned Parenthood's practices. Live Action's investigations of Planned Parenthood have fueled the effort at all levels of government to put an end to taxpayer dollars being given to the abortion giant, and most importantly, Lila's work has saved the lives of babies and inspired others to do the same.

...

The convergence of babies, political power, and justice is not new. In fact, this triumvirate of issues was central in the biblical account of Egypt's oppression of Israel (Exodus 1).

Knowing that the Bible is not just a compilation of great stories but a book of practical instruction on how to live (2 Timothy 3:16), what can we learn from Pharaoh's reaction to the Hebrews? the midwives' response to Pharaoh? God's reply to the midwives?

Evil prefers not to operate alone but to draft others into its service.

The Hebrew children were multiplying, and Pharaoh's reaction is characteristic of a leader who is insecure and therefore fearful of the future. Operating from this fear the leader, desperate to hold on to power, uses any means possible, including the murdering of innocent people. The twentieth century speaks clearly to this as dictators like Lenin, Hitler, Stalin, Pol Pot, and others murdered millions of their own citizens out of fear of losing power or for ideological reasons.

Evil prefers not to operate alone but to draft others into its service. In Pharaoh's case he called in the "Hebrew midwives" Shiphrah and Puah. Most Old Testament scholars suggest these two were Egyptians who were midwives to the Hebrew women, rather than Hebrew midwives. Some even suggest the two women were the heads of organizations that oversaw midwives, which is a reasonable conclusion considering the Hebrew population was estimated to be close to two million people at this point in history. It is even possible that Shiphrah and Puah were over portions of a government health-care system—maybe one was the secretary of labor!

The command from Pharaoh to the midwives was to kill the boy babies at birth, a form of sex selection, late-term abortion, or, more accurately, infanticide.

How did these midwives respond to Pharaoh?

While working among the Hebrew families, the midwives had apparently come to an understanding of God or possibly even have a relationship with Him. At a minimum the midwives placed a higher priority on the natural law established by God, which instructs that the killing of the innocent is wrong, than they did the fleeting edicts of Pharaoh. Whatever the source of their motivation, the result was that they had a greater fear of God than a fear of Pharaoh, so they refused to kill the Hebrew babies.

Keep in mind that refusing to comply with "Pharaoh Care" was no small matter. The risk they faced was much greater than an IRS audit or civil fines; they could lose not just their livelihood but their very lives.

They had a greater fear of God than a fear of Pharaoh, so they refused to kill the Hebrew babies.

Imagine the anxiety that must have enveloped them as they received a summons to Pharaoh's court. They were called onto the royal carpet and asked why they were letting the male children live. Read their response:

> Because the Hebrew women are not like the Egyptian
> women; for they are lively and give birth before the
> midwives come to them. (Exodus 1:19)

Was this claim true or were the midwives being deceptive?

It was probably true in some cases, but it is unlikely that it was true in all cases. If all the Hebrew women were giving birth without the aid of the midwives, then fear of God on behalf of the midwives (verse 17) would not have been necessary. In fact, this whole narrative could have been left out of this historical account.

The Bible makes clear the midwives acted in contravention to Pharaoh's orders, with the result being the lives of babies were saved and many Hebrew families enjoyed the blessings of life.

Some biblical scholars have struggled with the question of whether the actions of the midwives were justified or immoral. This is not an insignificant question considering what is happening in the US government with tax dollars going to the world's largest abortion provider, Planned Parenthood, and public policies that mandate taxpayer-funded abortion.

In determining the answer, we can look first at God's reply to the actions of the midwives: "Because the midwives feared [revered] God, he gave them families of their own" (verse 21, NIV).

Are we misreading this passage?

No, God blessed the midwives with the very object they helped the Hebrew women secure—families.

But should the midwives have been upfront with Pharaoh and told him to his face that they feared God more than him and that they were not going to be a part of his evil plan?

Possibly, but think about the potential consequences of directly confronting Pharaoh with their opposition from the outset. Such an approach may have put the lives of the midwives under their authority at risk, and it would have certainly not had the effect of sparing the lives of the children.

The midwives did not deceive Pharaoh for personal benefit or gain. In fact, they were taking a great personal risk to spare the lives of the Hebrew children. If it were about them, the midwives could have just maintained status quo and continued to enjoy their standing in the community by retaining the favor of Pharaoh and enjoying a politically connected and economically comfortable lifestyle.

The midwives were blessed, not for deceiving Pharaoh, but for having a greater fear of or reverence for God and for saving the innocent. It is important that we not see their actions as justified under a postmodern view of relative morality or situational ethics that says you can define right and wrong based upon the circumstances. There is justification here, but it flows from a biblical, objective view of morality that understands God's law is higher than man's (Acts 5:29).

In other words, if in the process of saving the Hebrew babies, out of a fear of acting against God, the midwives deceived and disobeyed a command from Pharaoh, which violated the moral law of God, their actions were justified. (This is the principle of the double effect explained by Thomas Aquinas in *Summa Theologiae*.)

Ultimately it is a question of whom we fear. The fear of man brings about cowardly actions that don't just target the innocent as Pharaoh did, but the fear of man causes many good people to shrink back in silence when they should speak out. On the other hand, the fear of or reverence for God elicits the courage to oppose evil and the schemes that are launched against the most innocent and defenseless among us.

MAKING IT REAL

1. Why is human life sacred and why should we protect it?
   Read Genesis 1:27.

2. Do you have an obligation to speak out for the innocent?
   Read Proverbs 24:11–12.

3. Not everyone is called to do what Lila Rose did in the battle
   against abortion. If you believe abortion is wrong, what
   would *you* be willing to do to save the lives of the unborn?
   What is your "fear level" when it comes to standing up for
   the unborn? How could your faith cancel out that fear?

4. Read Psalm 139:13–16 and consider God's love for you.
   Then pray and ask God to give you an understanding and
   love for all human life.

3

Too Pure for *American Idol*?

In 2001, a young girl with stars in her eyes traveled from her home in rural Texas to Los Angeles. Her goal: showbiz. Try and make it as a singer. As a teenager, she had starred in her high school's musicals and gotten scholarship offers from three schools, including the prestigious Berklee College of Music. Confident in her songwriting and singing skills, she turned down the offers, only to discover that the music business was tougher than she thought. After months of trying to secure a record deal, she returned to her hometown to wait tables.

When one of her friends suggested she enter a new talent contest called *American Idol,* she reluctantly auditioned. A few months later, Kelly Clarkson was crowned the winner of *American Idol's* premier season, and you know the rest of the story. An RCA mega record deal. Multiple Grammy awards. And a lot more money than she ever made waiting tables.

Is it any wonder that artists of varying degrees of talent would do *anything* to win over the judges on *American Idol*?

Which brings me to the story of Moriah Peters, an emerging talent in the Christian contemporary music scene. Like Kelly

Clarkson, Moriah turned down a college scholarship to pursue a music career. She also appeared on *American Idol,* but unlike Kelly, her audition didn't go so well, and that's what got my attention. But I'm getting a little ahead of myself.

Moriah's mom, raised by her grandmother in Mexico, grew up dirt poor and didn't speak English until she was twenty-one. Moriah's dad had it worse, barely surviving the tough streets of Pico Rivera, California. One of his earliest and enduring memories was seeing his dad punch his mom in the face and watching her spit broken teeth and blood into the palm of her hand. When he eventually met Patricia Castillo, it wasn't exactly a match made in heaven.

Or was it?

When God shows up, anything can happen. Patricia invited Jesus to be her Savior when she was in her midtwenties, and then she met Tony Peters. He fell pretty hard for her—how else could you explain why a guy who had never set foot in a church all of a sudden was sitting next to her every Sunday in the little congregation she attended? Turns out, Tony liked the music, and being a bass player, he asked the worship leader if he could join the praise band that led the congregation in worship. The leader asked him if he was a member, and upon discovering Tony wasn't, he made a strategic decision. He asked Tony, "What would happen if on your way home today you got in a wreck and were killed? Would you go to heaven or hell?"

Tony knew full well that he wasn't exactly heavenly material, and right then and there he asked the worship leader to show him how to become a Christian.

"I know that sounds corny," laughed Moriah when she shared this story with me. "But that's exactly how my dad accepted Jesus, and the transformation in his life proves that God can use any means to draw people into His family. Given the horrible conditions of his upbringing, he had every reason to become a horrible father, but he's the most God-fearing man I've ever known. My dad is my absolute hero!"

By the time Moriah came along, her dad had graduated from UCLA and earned his law degree from Loyola University. He eventually became one of the youngest judges in California history, but as far as Moriah is concerned, it is his faith—along with her mother's—that had the biggest impact on her.

When God shows up, anything can happen.

"I was fortunate to grow up in a Christian home with parents who loved God and clearly loved each other," Moriah observed. "But having a good Christian family doesn't make you a Christian; I had to make my own decisions about what I believed, and when I was in the sixth grade I had my first encounter with Jesus. I was at a church camp with my youth group, and one evening we were all lying on a hillside, looking up at the stars as someone played a guitar. In that moment, I imagined a big field with a stream flowing through it. Jesus was on the other side of the stream, and when I crossed over to His side, He just grabbed me, laughing, and swung me around. Up until then, I always thought God was unhappy with me, serious and stern. But for the first time I experienced Him as a loving friend. I guess you could say that, emotionally, I accepted Jesus as my Savior."

That worked for her in middle school, but high school was just around the corner, and we all remember high school, right? Trying to fit in and find your place. Plenty of "friends" who want to pull you into their little group, or mean kids who won't let you into theirs. For most kids trying to follow Jesus, high school is a nightmare, and it didn't help that Moriah had an influential English teacher who was an atheist and seemed hell-bent on challenging the fragile faith of any Christian in his class.

"He was a great teacher, extremely intelligent, the valedictorian of his graduating class at UCLA," Moriah recalled. "He asked a lot of tough questions and called me out along with my Christian friends, challenging our beliefs. To be honest, I didn't have any answers to his questions and began to experience a lot of doubts about my faith."

In her confusion, Moriah climbed to the patio roof at her home, looked up to the stars, and called out to a God she wasn't sure existed. The vastness of the dark sky and the silence of the night underscored her sense of smallness, insignificance. Even if there was a God out there, what did He care about a young, half-Mexican, half-French girl who was 100 percent confused?

"God, are You even real?" she whispered to the heavens. "I can't answer any of my teacher's questions. Nothing about You makes sense anymore."

For Moriah—and for many Christians—all the world's arguments supposedly based on logic and philosophy and science made more sense than her belief in a God she couldn't see. Her "emotional salvation" was enough for sixth grade, but it wasn't working in the real world of a public high school where Christianity was treated as a myth and Christians as fools. Sadly, it is in this environment that a lot of Christian kids cave, but Moriah wasn't about to.

"In spite of the fact that none of this Jesus thing made sense to me, I made a decision up there on the roof of our patio. I'm going to *choose* to believe. I'm going to trust. When it gets right down to it, we either choose to believe or we choose not to believe."

Despite being in a public school, Moriah found a teacher who let her start a small Bible study for girls in her classroom. Rather than go through all the red tape of trying to get approval from the administration, she just casually let a few friends know about it; and every Wednesday during lunch period, they would meet to study the Bible and pray. By the time she graduated, those Bible studies were standing-room only, as God honored her boldness.

> When it gets right down to it, we either choose to believe or we choose not to believe.

"Leading that Bible study became the foundation of my faith, where God showed me this was an opportunity for me to lead and be bold and that these are the people I am being called to reach—my peers. Sure, that atheist teacher and even other teachers tried to make me and other Christians look bad, but I wasn't in school to change *their* minds. I learned that being a Christian isn't about being right or winning, but serving the needs of others. God put these girls into my life because He loved them and wanted me to love them too. I also learned that if you take a stand for Jesus, yes, you need to be prepared for persecution, but you also have to be prepared to be a leader. People will flock to you. God will use you as a magnet for those who are struggling."

Fortunately, Moriah also had another huge resource for her growing faith: a strong church built on a foundation of biblical teaching. In fact, it was through her church that she honed her music talent, though for reasons unrelated to the possibility of turning that latent talent into a career.

"I had such an awful voice that my family nicknamed me Froggy," she laughed. "So when I was six, my parents had me take voice lessons from a woman at church, not because they wanted me to become a professional musician, but because they thought it would improve my low, scruffy voice."

As Moriah got older, she and a small group of friends began singing in church on special occasions like Easter and other holidays. They also led the worship time for the children's church, and it soon became clear that "Froggy's" voice wasn't froggy anymore. In fact Moriah's voice was the talk of the town. Friends from church and school began encouraging her to audition for *American Idol,* which she immediately dismissed.

"I'm the kind of girl that when someone tells me I should do something, I'm most likely going to do the opposite, so I pretty much was against the whole idea of trying out for *American Idol.* I didn't watch the show. I set my mind against it. I was sixteen years old and my sights were set on school—getting good enough grades to earn a scholarship to college. I had just gotten accepted into a law institute program at UCLA for high school students. My dream wasn't to be a musician but to become a lawyer. I thought that singing was just something you did on the side at church, not as a career."

Moriah may have blown off *American Idol,* but her mom . . . not so much. One morning as Moriah was about to leave for school, her entire family was sitting around the dining room table, and her mom held up a stack of papers.

"Moriah, here are the directions to the *American Idol* audition, here's the form you have to fill out and the instructions for what you have to do and the date for the audition. I've prayed about it, and I believe it's God's will that you do it, so we're going, and that's it."

One thing Moriah had learned long ago was that when her mom believed something was God's will, you didn't argue. So she reluctantly agreed to give it a try, which meant joining a few thousand other hopefuls at the Rose Bowl in Pasadena, California,

Friends from church and school began encouraging her to audition for *American Idol*.

for the first round of auditions. She stood in a slow-moving line of candidates that seemed a couple of miles long, stopping at various checkpoints along the way until finally, she got a very brief chance to sing in front of a group of *American Idol* staffers.

"With all those people trying to make it, I didn't really think I had much of a chance," Moriah told me. "Apparently they liked what they heard because I made it to the next round."

Making it only meant that she could move on to another audition. Of the thousands who show up to the initial audition in each city, only between one hundred and two hundred make it to the second round. The rest are sent home. To get to the big show in front of the celebrity judges, Moriah would have to get a thumbs-up from two more auditions, and each time the number who got selected got smaller and smaller. So a few weeks after making the first cut, she repeated the process all over again, and once again impressed the judges enough to have them send her to yet another audition. By now, she was getting excited about the whole thing, her confidence building with each small victory. The only hurdle between her and the celebrity judges was one more audition.

"When it came time for me to sing, I said a little prayer and gave it my best."

Her best was good enough. She nailed it! She was on to the next round, where she would almost certainly have the chance to perform in front of those celebrities, some of whom were known to make cruel comments. Who can forget Simon Cowell telling a contestant she sounded "like cats jumping off the Empire State Building"? And that was one of his kinder comments!

These were tough conditions for any artist, let alone one only sixteen years old. But the potential rewards were great. Consider the list of winners and finalists who went on to lucrative singing careers: Carrie Underwood, Jordin Sparks, Chris Daughtry, Fantasia Barrino, Ruben Studdard, and Jennifer Hudson. And of course, Kelly Clarkson. In fact, according to *Billboard Magazine,* the show has produced 345 chart-toppers from its ranks of winners and contestants, a fact that was not lost on Moriah.

"I'm not going to lie. There were moments when I thought, *Oh my gosh! I could be famous.* But at the same time, as we headed for the studios where I might make it to the televised audition, I had a real sense of peace. I felt spiritually prepared because I had so many people praying for me. My mom had got some women together, and during the audition process she would text them about how things were going. I knew they prayed for me nonstop throughout the whole thing. Sure I wanted to win, but even more important I wanted to honor God."

The final process was simple yet terrifying. Moriah and her parents drove to a two-story building along the water, where the contestants would first audition in front of producers on the first floor. Then if they made it past the producers, they would be sent up to the second floor to perform in front of the judges and cameras. To be this close and know that one wrong note, one missed beat, and you're done can do a number on your confidence. Having her parents there and knowing that she was covered with prayer meant a lot to Moriah, but God sent her another comforting message from an unlikely source.

When it came time for me to sing, I said a little prayer and gave it my best.

"After I sang in front of the producers, I was sent to a room to wait. There was a lot of waiting that day, which is not exactly relaxing. Normally I would have been a hot mess of nerves, but over in the corner of the room was a group of gospel singers who were also competing. They were quietly singing worship songs, so I went over to that corner to join them and just worshiped with them. It was so amazing—here we were in the midst of this cultural, spiritual battle. I'm sure they wanted to win as badly as I did, but our faith brought us together. It was as if God was reminding us: *You're not alone. I'm right here with you.*"

Word soon came from the producers that she had made it! She would be going upstairs to perform for the celebrity judges. The little brown-eyed girl who used to sing in children's church would now sing into the homes of the millions of viewers who had made *American Idol* one of the most-watched shows on television.

"Someone took me up to this huge room with floor-to-ceiling windows on one side and in the middle of one of the walls, a set of double doors. I knew what was behind those doors. Cameras to catch every expression as I stepped out in front of the celebrity panel. Ryan Seacrest, waiting to introduce me. It was pretty exciting and nerve wracking because completely lining the room were the people I would be competing against, all sitting in chairs awaiting their opportunity to try and hit the big time. As each contestant walked through the doors to audition, we would all slide over to the next chair as we waited for our turn. Pretty soon, there were only a few contestants ahead of me and I found myself sitting with the double doors to my left and the windows right in front of me. I knew I would be going through those doors soon and started to get a little bit nervous. The room was thick with tension—you could feel it. But as I looked out those windows and saw the beautiful blue sky and how expansive it was, the Lord reminded me that He's omnipotent; He has everything under control. And in that moment I said, 'God, You've got this.' I immediately felt at peace, which was sort of funny because a woman right next to me was literally having a panic attack, something I had never seen before."

Soon, Moriah found herself sitting in the last chair next to the double doors. Knowing that in minutes she would be in front of the judges almost took her breath away. She stood and waited for the producer to give her the signal. She could almost feel her heart beating in her throat. Each contestant had been given a list of about two hundred songs that they could choose from, and she had chosen "Angel." It was the only song that included a reference to heaven, and she loved being able to sing about it. But what if she stumbled? What if she forgot the words, something that had happened with previous contestants?

When the doors opened, it was as if Moriah had always sung before millions. She walked confidently to her spot on the audition floor and treated the judges and America to a beautiful rendition of the song made famous by Jessica Simpson. And just like that, it was over.

Almost. Time for the judges' comments.

At every level of audition, contestants are interviewed by a panel, and the transcripts of each interview of those who make it to the celebrity stage are given to the judges. So by now, these judges knew Moriah's entire life story. One of the things she consistently focused on in her interviews was the fact that she felt called to purity in her life and that when she was fourteen she decided that she wanted to save her first kiss for her wedding day.

"The comments started out great," Moriah recalled. "They told me they loved my voice and that my look was great. It was pretty flattering. But then they started in on how I wanted to save my first kiss until I was married. They thought that was pretty odd. Avril Lavigne was a guest judge that day and she said, 'I think you're just trying to be too perfect.' And then Kara DioGuardi said, "You just need to go out in the world and make mistakes and get some life experience. Maybe you should go kiss a guy because there's something about kissing that makes you feel sexy. Then after you kiss someone, come back and audition for us.' After they said all those things, I realized that this was the Lord closing the door for me. It was His will."

> I realized that this was the Lord closing the door for me. It was His will.

Contestants were prepped ahead of time to make a big scene if they didn't make it to the next round, and Moriah didn't make it.

"I'll admit I was pretty disappointed, but God gave me the strength to use this disappointment for His honor. Someone put a microphone in front of me and asked me how I felt, and I was able to say, 'God opened doors for me to get this far and then closed them, and I'm not going to question it because I know He has bigger things for me.'"

The cameras trailed Moriah all the way down through the building and into the parking lot, trying to get a reaction that would make what they consider to be great TV. Moriah allowed herself a little fun in spite of her disappointment.

"One of them asked, 'Are you going to go out and kiss a guy now?' I reminded them that I was still planning to wait until I was married and since I was only sixteen, they might have to wait awhile to get that shot."

After the cameras left, it was just Moriah and her parents in the parking lot. In her heart, Moriah knew that what had just happened was God's will—that He was in control of everything. But there was a part of her that was confused and hurt: Why would God let her get so close and then close the door? Why would her godly commitment to purity stand in the way of possibly landing a big record deal?

As they walked toward their car, a man approached them.

"Excuse me," he began. "I was in the audition waiting room and heard you sing through the closed doors. You have a beautiful voice, and I heard what you said on camera about God. I'm a believer and I really want to introduce you to someone."

That someone was Wendy Green, whose husband is a producer in Nashville and the musical director for the well-known artist Steven Curtis Chapman. Moriah and her parents met with Wendy, and after the meeting Wendy casually said that God had told her to help Moriah get a record deal in Nashville. Within a matter of weeks, Moriah and her dad flew to Nashville where working with Wendy's husband she wrote songs and recorded a demo that they would send around to record labels. It was pretty heavy stuff for the newly turned seventeen-year-old, and on the way back to L.A., it hit her.

"I knew how hard it was to get a record deal, and I had so little to offer. I didn't have a library of songs. Nobody knew me. I didn't even have a Twitter account, so I had no followers. I wasn't exactly what record labels were looking for."

Then there was that other part of her life. Her dream to become a lawyer. She not only had been accepted into UCLA's honors program, but her education would be paid for by the scholarship they offered. It was a great situation—everything that she had worked so hard for was right there in front of her.

> I needed God to make it obvious to me what I should do.

"I told God, 'If You want me to move to Nashville and try to do music, You're going to have to make it crystal clear to me that that's Your will because I don't think I have enough faith to step out in the dark.' I had heard countless stories of people who had moved to Nashville, leaving everything behind to wait tables and work at coffee shops and do whatever it takes to get recognized or signed, but I couldn't do that. I needed God to make it obvious to me what I should do."

In a matter of days after praying that prayer, Moriah got a call from Wendy.

"Moriah, you have to come back to Nashville. Every single label who has your demo wants to make an offer."

Remember back when Moriah was on the patio roof,

wondering if God was real? Despite her doubts and uncertainty, she chose to believe that Jesus is the Son of God who offered her the free gift of salvation. When God made it clear that He wanted her to return to Nashville, she obeyed and soon after she got there, she signed on with Reunion Records, joining fellow artists Steven Curtis Chapman, Brandon Heath, and Casting Crowns. And the title of her first album?

I Choose Jesus.

Oh, and one of the men she was introduced to was Joel Smallbone, from the Christian band For King & Country. Joel served as a co-producer for *I Choose Jesus* and enjoys the honor of being the very first man that Moriah ever kissed.

After they married on July 7, 2013.

"Marrying Joel was the most beautiful day of my life. And every day since then has confirmed that we were made for each other."

How cool is that?

I have to admit, I've never liked the name *American Idol.* Whenever I hear the name, I can't help but hear God's repeated warnings against serving any other god but the one true God. You think it was easy for Moriah Peters to talk about purity and not kissing a guy until she was married? On television? In front of the very people who could reward her with fame and fortune? It wasn't. But it was the right thing to do.

The Bible encourages us to "not become weary in doing good, for at the proper time we will reap a harvest if we do not give up" (Galatians 6:9, NIV). Moriah could have decided to leave her faith and values out of her interviews, and I could make a case that had she done that she might be in a vastly different place today. But not a better place.

Today, Moriah fills arenas with fans drawn to her unique voice and all-in heart for God. But it hasn't all been rosy. Life is messy, even for Christians. Soon after their marriage, while on tour, Moriah became ill and was hospitalized.

"The doctors initially believed that I might have leukemia, and that scared me in a way I'd never been scared before."

After days of prayer, doctors diagnosed her illness as an unknown virus that currently remains a mystery.

"I learned a valuable lesson during those moments when I didn't have strength to speak. Life can't be taken for granted, no matter what your age. I also understood that fear and faith often come in a package. Choosing faith is an act of bravery."

Life can't be taken for granted, no matter what your age.

Regardless of what you might think it costs to stand up to the pressure to conform to the world's values, caving in will never pay off. By the way, Moriah's newest album is called *Brave*.

Makes perfect sense to me.

■■■

Kansas governor Sam Brownback is a personal friend of mine, and I remember an occasion visiting with him in his office during his time in the US Senate. I don't recall what we were discussing, but I do remember seeing in his private office a Post-it note on the mirror that read "Just Hug Jesus!"

Hug Jesus? What does that mean? Well, think about it: when you are really hugging someone, it's hard to hold on to anything else.

Moriah Peters, like Abraham, learned that you had to be willing to let some things go if you were going to wholeheartedly embrace the Lord.

Abraham finally had what he had wanted almost his entire life, a son—a son of his own. He had waited a long time. In fact, Hebrews says that when Isaac was born Abraham was so old he was "as good as dead" (Hebrews 11:12). Now that's pretty old! Abraham was beginning to see the realization of God's promise that was made to him years before when God had said, "I will make you a great nation" (Genesis 12:2).

Do you think Abraham replayed those words over in his mind a few times as he began his journey to a land that God said He would show him? As he walked across the vast desert landscape looking into the night sky illuminated by the countless stars in the heavens, he had to wonder how God could make a great nation out of a childless couple. I would venture to say that Abraham had a Post-it parchment on the tent wall reminding himself of what God had said and reminding himself that he had chosen to believe.

It was all starting to come together. With the birth of a son, the wondering was over. It might take a while with just one son, but Abraham was no doubt counting on Isaac growing up and providing Grandpa Abraham lots of grandchildren. Then came the test that went beyond anything Abraham had ever faced.

Leaving the land of Ur behind or facing the retribution of kings and pharaohs seemed insignificant in light of what God was calling him to do now.

"Take now your son, your only son Isaac, whom you love, and go to the land of Moriah, and offer him there as a burnt offering on one of the mountains of which I shall tell you" (Genesis

22:2). I could imagine Abraham responding with, "Whoa! Where did that come from? That can't possibly be God. I'll never realize the promise if I let go of my only son! Can you imagine what others are going to think? By the way, God, did You tell Sarah about this?"

That's not what Abraham said. In fact, he didn't say anything; he didn't try to rationalize or justify disobeying God. Just as he had chosen to believe Him, he now chose to obey Him, no questions asked.

When came the test that went beyond anything Abraham had ever faced.

"So Abraham rose early in the morning and saddled his donkey, and took two of his young men with him, and Isaac his son; and he split the wood for the burnt offering, and arose and went to the place of which God had told him" (verse 3).

While we see this now as the vivid imagery of what God the Father did for us on the wood formed into a cross by giving His only Son as a sacrifice for our sin, Abraham's perspective was one-dimensional. Abraham was living it. It was his son, his only son that God had promised him, that he was now being told to offer as a sacrifice.

It is hard to even begin to comprehend the emotions Abraham must have felt. That three-day journey to Mount Moriah had to have been the longest three days of Abraham's life as he pondered what lay before him. But he did not waver.

Abraham was so confident in the promise of God that the writer of Hebrews said, "By faith Abraham, when he was tested, offered up Isaac, and he who had received the promises offered up his only begotten son, of whom it was said, 'In Isaac your seed shall be called,' concluding that God was able to raise him up, even from the dead, from which he also received him in a figurative sense" (Hebrews 11:17–19).

At the moment that Abraham let go of the very dream that God had given him, the breakthrough came and one of the greatest examples of God's grace and provision was demonstrated. It was the same for Moriah, at the moment she chose to embrace Jesus and let go of the dream of being an *American Idol* star—God provided!

MAKING IT REAL

1. Where are you in your journey? Has God given you a dream, a vision that you are pursuing?

2. Has your passion for your dream replaced your passion for God? Sometimes there is very little difference between a dream and an idol. God wants all of your devotion.

3. Is God calling you to let go of what you are holding on to and "just hug Jesus"? Let go of it and God will be your provider.

4. Is something holding you back from embracing Jesus and giving everything to Him? Then pray and ask the Lord to make Deuteronomy 11:22–23 a reality in your life: "For if you carefully keep all these commandments which I command you to do—to love the LORD your God, to walk in all His ways, and to hold fast to Him—then the LORD will drive out all these nations from before you, and you will dispossess greater and mightier nations than yourselves."

4

Silencing Fear

Roy was running late, and a thousand thoughts and emotions were running through his mind as he turned onto Highway 123 for the twenty-five-minute drive to Littlejohn Coliseum on the Clemson campus. This was graduation day, a day for Roy to celebrate the accomplishments of him and his classmates. The day held extra significance for Roy, as he was the class valedictorian. But unbeknownst to his closest friends and even members of his own family, Roy Costner IV would face a test on this day that would cause all those academic examinations to pale in comparison. This would be a test of what the eighteen-year-old really believed. And whom he really feared.

Just months earlier, Roy's hometown of Liberty, South Carolina, population 3,269, was swept into the anti-religious freedom campaign of a Wisconsin-based atheist organization called the Freedom From Religion Foundation (FFR). The organization had a clear modus operandi: target schools and local governments in rural communities, which are typically underfunded and therefore fearful of lawsuits. Pick on the little guys and they'll cave in to FFRF's demands. The Pickens County school board, which oversees twenty-six schools, including Liberty High School where Roy was a senior, received a letter from FFRF demanding they change their policies on prayer to comply with what can only be described as the militant anti–religious freedom agenda of FFRF or face being dragged into court.

The truth is FFRF rarely goes to court and legal victories for them are even rarer. But unfortunately, they have found great success through bullying and intimidating rural governments, primarily in the South. These small communities are usually overtly Christian in their civic life—it's not unusual to attend a civic event that begins with an invocation. But when organizations like FFRF flex their muscles, these salt-of-the-earth people usually back down before the matter ever makes it into a court of law.

In November 2012 the Pickens County board of trustees received their first letter from Patrick Elliott, staff attorney with FFRF, complaining about prayer at their monthly meetings.

> It is our information and understanding that the SDPC Board of Trustees (Board) begins its monthly meetings with invocation. . . . In fact, a [*sic*] SDPC student typically leads the invocation. These prayers have included references to the "Holy Spirit" and often ended with "in Jesus' name we pray," or other reference to Jesus. . . . We ask that you take immediate action and refrain from scheduling prayers as part of future Board of Trustees meetings. We further ask that you revise SDPC policies to comport with the U.S. Constitution. Please respond in writing with the steps you are taking to remedy this constitutional violation.

The board of trustees responded in part to the letter by seeking a legal opinion from the South Carolina attorney general. The AG stopped short of saying the board had to cease all prayer as FFRF was demanding, recommending the school board adopt a policy of opening their session with nonsectarian prayers like those offered at the openings of other legislative bodies. So, on February 25, after studying the matter, the board was prepared to entertain a motion that would establish a nonsectarian prayer policy with members of the board opening each meeting in prayer.

FFRF fired off another letter saying the proposal would not suffice. Again, writing for FFRF, staff attorney Patrick Elliott wrote, "While the board has heard from a number of County residents who support school prayer, it must not heed to a religious majority." Elliott went on to increase FFRF's demands, insisting that the board "drop [all] religious rituals from its official duties."

When the board's public meeting began at 7:00 p.m., the administrative office at the Pickens County school board reflected both the tension and interest in the subject. Incensed that an out-of-state atheist organization was trying to dictate how they would live, over one thousand students, parents, and other citizens spilled out of the hearing room into the hallways and foyer, and dozens more gathered in circles around the perimeter of the building praying for the trustees and the meeting.

Nineteen citizens, young and old, spoke in favor of retaining the long-standing policy protecting the free exercise of religion in Pickens County. Speaker after speaker made clear that students and others should not have to check their faith at the door of the school or any other governmental building for that matter. This was America, a nation built on religious freedom. Not a single person spoke in support of the proposed actions being considered by the board that had resulted from FFRF's demand letter. The clerk read the board's proposed policy:

> The board is a deliberative body and will open its regular public meetings with a public invocation complying with Section 6-1-160 of the Code of Laws of South Carolina. The board will not begin meetings for student matters with a public invocation.
>
> The public invocation will be nonsectarian and will not proselytize for or advance any one, or disparage any other, faith or belief. The public invocation is for the benefit of the board but no member of the board, or any other person attending the meeting, will be required to participate in the public invocation. The purposes of the public invocation are to express thankfulness for the right of self-government, solemnize the board's legislative tasks, dignify and confirm the seriousness of board meetings, encourage respect and appreciation for all board members, seek to unite and not divide the board, and contribute to the wisdom and soundness of decisions by the board.
>
> The public invocation will be offered on a voluntary basis by a member of the board, rotating from meeting to meeting, in alphabetical order, or other objective method of rotation, among all members of the board. A board member may offer a moment of silence for silent prayer or reflection in addition to or in lieu of the public invocation.

In other words, "prayer" would be reduced to a few kind words expressed to no one in particular. Many of the citizens gathered there that evening knew this policy would dramatically change this deeply religious and God-fearing community. Eliminating real prayer from school-board meetings would not only remove one of the final tokens of their collective acknowledgment of God, it would lead to fewer freedoms for the district's sixteen thousand students.

The tension mounted in the packed hearing room as the board moved toward a vote. As expected, the board capitulated.

"Motion carries with three in favor, two opposed, and one abstention," the clerk stated.

Although he did not testify that night at the meeting, Roy was in the crowd and couldn't believe what had just happened.

"I knew that every aspect of Christian life would change," he recalled. "My teachers used to show up at extracurricular activities where prayer or religion were involved, but that vote changed everything. Events such as 'See You at the Pole,' the annual student-led prayer gathering, would now be strictly off limits to our teachers and other school personnel."

> **P**rayer would be reduced to a few kind words expressed to no one in particular.

Earlier, in August 2011, Roy and a couple of his friends had launched a web-based news and information site called Liberty Speaks.net. As with most new media initiatives, they designed it to counter the negative one-sided stories in the local "mainstream" press.

Liberty Speaks weighed deeper into the controversy as FFRF, emboldened by the board's capitulation, advanced their assault.

In an April letter, FFRF demanded action against Chris Carter, the athletic director at nearby Easley High School, for commenting that the new head football coach was a Christian. Additionally, they demanded action against an elementary-school teacher who had allowed Christian praise music in the classroom. They complained about posters that had apparent "Christian" references that were found in one school. However, it would be Liberty High School's graduation where the controversy would reach its crescendo.

Three weeks before graduation, Principal Lori Gwinn informed Roy that he would be Liberty High School's valedictorian for 2013.

"I was kind of surprised because having the highest grade-point average seemed pretty remote," Roy explained. "Obviously, I was thrilled to receive this honor, but it didn't take long before I realized I would be right in the center of the district-wide controversy over prayer that had been initiated less than six months ago."

My first reaction was "No way!" Principal Gwinn made clear that under the newly adopted policies of the board of trustees, there would be no prayer at the commencement ceremony and that there could be no references to God or religion in the speeches or comments from the students.

"My first reaction was 'No way!' I was not about to let some group of outsiders keep me from praying at my graduation. But then I began to question my motivation. Was I responding out of anger with a desire to make a statement, or was I acting out of a desire to please the Lord?"

In the emotion and high-level stress surrounding what should have been a festive occasion, Roy couldn't answer that question.

Instead, he began to pray, seeking guidance and direction for a decision that could have significant consequences for him and his family. A self-described procrastinator, Roy waited until just a little over one week from graduation to prepare his speech, which had to be approved by Principal Gwinn.

Roy's first draft included not only multiple references to God but also the Lord's Prayer. Knowing that would never fly, Roy removed the prayer and left only one reference to God before submitting the speech for approval. Principal Gwinn notified him that his speech, with the phrase "I am happy that both my parents led me to the Lord," had been approved.

Even with an approved speech in hand, Roy was still waiting for an answer from the Lord on whether or not he should say the Lord's Prayer. Should he be silent and allow God to be driven out of a public event in a community that overwhelmingly supported the freedom of religious expression? More significantly, would he deny who he was and the faith that was central to his life?

More significantly, would he deny who he was and the faith that was central to his life?

Prayer holds great significance to the Costner family. In fact, they attribute Roy's very existence to prayer. Born nearly two months premature, he was not expected to live. Roy's mother, Angie, was diagnosed with HELLP syndrome, a life-threatening obstetric complication that usually begins in the third trimester. Upon diagnosis, the doctors informed Roy's dad that the prospects for his wife and son were not good and that it was unlikely they would both survive.

Roy's dad—Roy Sr.—immediately reached out to the prayer

warriors at their church, and word then began to spread through prayer chains across the nation. After several emotionally and spiritually taxing weeks, Roy Sr. took his wife and newborn son home, their prayers answered.

Having been birthed and sustained through prayer, Roy didn't know any other way of life. But at ten years of age, Roy realized that growing up in a Christian home was not enough to secure his own eternal destiny. The faith of his father had to become his own faith, and for Roy it did. Listening to Josh McDowell's testimony at a youth conference in Gatlinburg, Tennessee, Roy knew something was missing. Upon returning home, he spoke with his dad, the two of them prayed together, and Roy made Jesus Christ his personal Savior and Lord.

How can I deny not only who I am, but whose I am? Roy asked himself as the passage from Matthew 10:33 kept coming to mind: *"But whoever denies Me before men, him I will also deny before My Father who is in heaven."*

In seeking to obtain a clear answer, Roy sought the counsel of his dad, who serves as the worship leader at their church and has discipled Roy from a young age. His advice to his son: "Make sure whatever you do, you do it for the right reason."

Roy also spoke with his pastor, Chad Hope, and Scott Uselman, the senior pastor at Smith Chapel where Roy attended as a young boy. While both echoed his father's caution about motives, they both encouraged him to publicly stand for the Lord.

As the weight of the moment settled upon the Costner household the night before the commencement ceremony, Roy again contemplated his motives and the potential consequences of his actions. His dad once again simply asked, "Son, are you doing this for political purposes or out of revenge toward the school, or are you doing this because God is such an important part of your life and this is what He is leading you to do?"

At that point Roy had his answer. His course was set.

Roy pulled into the parking lot at Littlejohn Coliseum and finished off the last of his Monster drink, then quickly exited his car and stepped into what was a hotter-than-normal Saturday for May.

The other students were already lined up in a long hallway outside the arena floor preparing to walk in, when

Roy's heart began to race faster and faster as he thought about what lay just ahead.

Roy dashed through the double doors as he pulled on his robe and took his designated spot in line as valedictorian. As "Pomp and Circumstance" began to play over the sound system and the procession moved slowly forward, Roy's heart began to race faster and faster as he thought about what lay just ahead. He was fighting against the fear and doubts that came as he once again considered the possible repercussions:

Will I lose my diploma? Can they really keep me from graduating? What else can they do to me?

There was also a little fear of repeating something that happened years before when he tripped in front of an auditorium filled with kids at the beginning of a pep rally.

There would be no tripping today. Roy took his place on the front row, waiting for his first assignment, as his classmates filed in. In addition to giving the traditional valedictorian speech, Roy was also responsible for leading the gathering in the Pledge of Allegiance. Nervous he might stumble over a word or two in the pledge, he found himself encouraged when the volume of the voices rose distinctively louder as hundreds of the friends and family who were in attendance for this special day practically shouted the words "under God." The still-brewing controversy sparked by the Freedom From Religion Foundation had not escaped those attending Liberty High School's graduation.

Following the pledge, Roy took his seat once again on the front row next to R. J. Little, the class salutatorian, who Roy had actually thought would be the valedictorian. The program agenda now transitioned to award presentations.

"As my classmates went up to get their awards, I could feel the butterflies fluttering in my stomach, and my heart began to race," Roy recounted. "I knew once the awards were handed out, I was next."

Principal Gwinn called Roy to the platform and gave him a glowing introduction. As she spoke, all he could think about was how the audience would respond to his speech. He didn't have long to find out.

As he stepped behind the podium, his prepared speech was in the "official" binder on the podium. After greeting everyone he made reference to the process and the fact that he had submitted his speech to Principal Gwinn.

"I first wanted to say that I turned my speech into Mrs. Gwinn, which she approved," he told the crowd. "Obviously, that means I did not do my job, so we're going to use a different one."

At that point he pulled the approved speech from the binder and ripped the paper in half, then pulled another speech from the sleeve of his robe. You could hear the gasps across the audience and see puzzled looks on the faces of the faculty seated behind Roy.

Continuing, Roy recognized several members of his class for their outstanding contributions to the football team, band, and drama. Then he proceeded to talk about how "the people who mentored us, those we look up to, they have helped carve and mold us into the young adults we are today. I am so thankful that both of my parents led me to the Lord," Roy said.

Then came the moment. Roy shuffled his feet and verbally paused with a long "and" as he put aside the last-minute hesitations and transitioned. "I think most of you will understand when I say, 'Our Father, who art in heaven hallowed be Thy name . . .'" As members of the faculty shifted in their seats uncomfortably, the audience began to applaud.

As members of the faculty shifted in their seats uncomfortably, the audience began to applaud.

Roy continued, "Thy kingdom come . . ." At this point Roy could hardly hear his own voice over the applause and shouts of affirmation from the audience.

"Thy will be done on earth as it is in heaven. Give us this daily our daily bread and forgive us our trespasses as we forgive those who trespass against us." Roy kept a normal cadence in his words as the audience quieted down for the final lines of the prayer.

"Lead us not into temptation, but deliver us from evil," he said as he momentarily stepped back preparing for the conclusion of the prayer.

With his right hand extended heavenward, Roy said with great emphasis, "For thine is the kingdom, the power and the glory, forever and ever, Amen."

This was the opportunity many in the community had waited for, to stand with someone who was not afraid to challenge those who were robbing them of their God-given First Amendment freedoms.

The coliseum erupted in extended applause, cheering, and shouts of support. Roy had made his choice: to fear God, not man.

While making the choice and carrying through with it brought a sense of relief and even peace, Roy was still uncertain of what actions school officials might take as he sat through the remainder of the graduation ceremony. He was about to find out.

Immediately following the ceremony, a member of the faculty approached Roy and said that while he couldn't say anything publicly, he appreciated the stand Roy had taken. Another said she agreed with Roy and hoped other students would have the same courage in the future. Even a member of the board of trustees thanked Roy for his stance. Roy had his diploma and there would be no retaliation from the school.

Roy was given an even greater platform to stand for his faith in Jesus Christ.

But the matter wasn't over.

Roy's graduation prayer went viral and became one of the latest examples of the effort of the secularists to remake America in their image. While most of the liberal media ignored it, the conservative media outlets gave the story plenty of attention; and Roy, far from being silenced as the FFRF had hoped, was given an even greater platform to stand for his faith in Jesus Christ.

All because he refused to bow to the demands of those who want to destroy religious freedom.

■ ■ ■

Now when Daniel knew that the writing was signed, he went home. And in his upper room, with his windows

> open toward Jerusalem, he knelt down on his knees three
> times that day, and prayed and gave thanks before his
> God, as was his custom since early days. (Daniel 6:10)

Not only had Daniel survived a change in administrations, he was promoted to one of the three presidents or chief overseers under Darius, the Mede king who defeated the Chaldeans and killed Belshazzar in 539 BC, whom Daniel had also served. Darius must have been impressed with the wisdom and résumé of Daniel to have picked a captive from the conquered region of Jerusalem as his top ruler. The words written by Solomon some four hundred years before explain the selection well: "Do you see a man who excels in his work? He will stand before kings; he will not stand before unknown men" (Proverbs 22:29).

Daniel is a great example of how God exalts those who faithfully serve Him even in the most hostile of environments. But this blessing and promotion by God does not come without detractors. Shortly after the promotion party, the other members of the triumvirate and a number of the regional leaders began looking for dirt on Daniel with the purpose of having him removed or at least diminishing his influence with Darius, which appeared to be significant. Nothing could be found. Daniel was above reproach.

Daniel 6:5 says, "Then these men said, 'We shall not find any charge against this Daniel unless we find it against him concerning the law of his God.'" In other words, "We've got to find a way to turn his devotion to his God, which has apparently prospered him, into a liability."

Their scheming minds devised a plan. Stoke the king's ego and get him to sign a royal, irreversible, nonamendable statute that declares that no one within the kingdom can petition any god or man but King Darius for thirty days. It worked and he signed it. The overt persecution and prosecution of followers of the one true God was now a national policy. See a parallel to today's America?

How did Daniel respond? Did he comply? Did he shrink back and hide his faith? No. Daniel, though a captive in a foreign land, feared God more than any man. Yes, he had a lot to lose, chiefly his life since this was a capital offense, but he was more fearful of displeasing the One who had saved him than one who had the power to kill him.

"Now when Daniel knew that the writing was signed, he went home. And in his upper room, with his windows open toward Jerusalem, he knelt down on his knees three times that day, and prayed and gave thanks before his God, as was his custom since early days" (verse 10).

You know the rest of the story. The conspirators now had what they needed. They took the evidence to Darius, and the king reluctantly complied and had Daniel placed in the lions' den. After spending a sleepless and restless night, the king was all too happy when God shut the mouths of the lions and delivered Daniel, his trusted servant, alive and well. Those seeking to ensnare Daniel were then thrown into the pit they had planned for Daniel, and the king declared what is latent in the heart of every human: there is a God that is above all, who is to be feared.

There are a few key aspects of Daniel's response that are instructive to us in the increasingly similar times in which we find ourselves today, where there is tolerance for almost everything but devotion to the one true God.

First, Daniel fully perceived the significance of the conspiracy against him and the pending consequences for praying to God, yet he did not yield to the political or cultural pressure. Why?

Daniel had a greater fear of not pleasing God than he had a fear of the displeasure of the latest king on the scene. God had established a track record in Daniel's life. Over and over, from the very beginning when he was taken captive as a youth in 605 BC, Daniel had found God's favor as he was faithful to God. Similar to how David recounted God's deliverance from the lion and the bear in order to gain confidence to face Goliath, Daniel was confident in the hand of God to protect him from the harms of this world or to promote him to the next. But regardless, he would not deny Him.

God shut the mouths of the lions and delivered Daniel, his trusted servant, alive and well.

What's your track record with God?

Each time we face one of these spiritual "bears" or "lions," our faith in God increases. But we have to be faithful to God to experience His intervening favor.

Secondly, the character of Daniel's prayer is very instructive: it's courageously conspicuous. Daniel continued what was his custom, praying three times a day. Herein lies the key to his courage. He wasn't making a political statement; he was exercising what our own founding fathers recognized as an inalienable right that comes not from government but from God—the liberty to worship God. Daniel had the courage to stand before men because he bowed before God, not just when the heat was on, but from the moment he saw the light of God's grace as a youth.

His public prayer was not a statement of defiance against the king, but a statement of dependence upon *the* King. In Daniel's day, as our own, the political and cultural environment was clearly hostile toward those who sought to live out their faith in the one true God. Daniel was not seeking to impose his religion on anyone, but rather he simply desired and expected accommodation for his faith. Despite what the secularists and militant anti-Christians claim, seeking the right to pray in public— whether you are a principal, a student, or a politician—is not an attempt to impose religion on a community or the country; it is exercising our God-given rights to live out our faith in a real and tangible way.

What is actually taking place is that the secularists of our day are just like those who were plotting against Daniel: they are trying to *exclude* the worship of the true God from public space. The reason is they are fearful that the power of the truth will lead, as it did in Daniel's day, to the universal acknowledgment of the dominion of God.

And finally, Daniel prevailed and, as a result, prospered as he confidently relied, not upon his own power or political connections, but upon the omnipotence of God. With a heart of gratitude he bowed before God, even as the lions roared, because Daniel knew the key to silencing fear.

Do you have that kind of relationship with your heavenly Father? If not, you can.

MAKING IT REAL

1. Have you, like Roy Costner, ever felt pressured to keep silent about your belief in Jesus? How do you usually respond?

2. What would you do if a teacher or principal told you that you could not wear a T-shirt with a Bible verse on it?

3. Why do you think expressions of Christian faith have come under pressure from local governments?

4. What's the difference between openly acknowledging your faith in Christ and imposing your faith on others?

5

Laid Back Doesn't Mean Lying Down

Sometimes I'm not sure what's worse: threats of physical violence against people who take a stand for God, or the more common practice of ridiculing with the intent of marginalizing people who refuse to compromise their Christian beliefs. Sticks and stones may indeed break bones, but words *can* hurt too. Regardless of how old you are, we all like to fit in. To be liked. No one wants to be labeled with some derogatory and hateful name, singled out by the rest of the crowd for the sake of everyone else's amusement. And that's especially true in high school, where everything from the clothes you wear to the style of your hair to the music you listen to must meet the approval of whatever group you belong to. The last thing you want to be in high school is different, which is why high school should have been a blast for Chad Farnan.

Chad pretty much fit in. The stereotypical Southern California laid-back surfer look. Tall. Athletic. Easygoing. When he wasn't in the pool training with his swim team, he was at the beach hanging out with his friends or working out—the sun and chlorine producing what his midwestern counterparts sought in claustrophobic booths and "product": perpetually tanned and blond. A good student supported by a great family, Chad was sailing through high school as a popular, well-adjusted student-athlete, the last guy you would expect to become the victim of bullying. And you won't believe who the bully was.

"Growing up, my life was pretty ordinary," Chad told me. "I've lived in the same house in Mission Viejo since the day I was born. We lived in a good neighborhood, had a stable family life. I always enjoyed school and did pretty well because I studied hard. But I also had a lot of friends and we had fun together."

His parents, Bill and Teresa, took Chad and his older sister to church occasionally, but in the early years, faith wasn't central to their lives. That is, until they found a new church whose teachings never strayed from the Bible. It was at Foothill Family Church where Chad and his family recognized their need to make Jesus the Lord of their lives.

"It was really neat because our entire family began to grow in our faith together. I was still pretty young—a sixth grader—but I realized what Jesus had done for me on the cross and decided I wanted to follow Him for the rest of my life. I got pretty involved with my church and youth group. Our youth leader introduced me to a series of devotionals written by Kenneth Hagin, and I just devoured them. I read them over and over again to the point they started to wear out."

Just as he was beginning to take his faith seriously, he began pursuing sports with the same focus and fervor. A friend introduced him to water polo, and from that point on he spent most of his spare time in the pool.

"From about the seventh grade on through college, I was passionate about water polo and swimming and spent all my time competing or training for both sports. Every morning I'd get up early and go to practice, then go to my classes, and then it was back in the pool again after school. And the next morning, get up and do it all over again."

In the classroom, Chad kept his head above water, but acknowledged his devotion to sports was not matched by his interest in academics. Still, as a student-athlete he kept his grades up—mostly Bs and the occasional C.

"To be honest, in high school I was all about sports."

I don't know about you, but when I think of a teenager courageous enough to take a stand on principles or convictions, I think of some overachieving, deeply intense individual who seems destined for greatness—willing and ready to respond to whatever challenge life presents. Yet here was a guy we might jokingly refer to as a jock, not really setting the world on fire in the classroom, sailing through life without a whole lot of worries or concerns. Fully devoted to God, yet not set on some strategic plan to change the world. Can God use an ordinary guy like Chad Farnan to take a stand for His kingdom? Chad was about to find out.

To be honest, in high school I was all about sports.

As a sophomore, Chad had signed up for AP (advanced placement) European history, taught by James Corbett, a popular though somewhat eccentric teacher. Though not necessarily required for those planning on attending college, it was one of those classes your counselor told you to take if you wanted to do well in college. It's safe to say that for the fifteen years Mr. Corbett had taught the class, nearly every student from Capistrano Valley High School who went on to college took the course. Chad would be one of them. At least for a while.

On the first day of the new semester, Chad waited outside in the warm Southern California sun until the absolute last minute, then raced off to class. Like every other student beginning a new school year, the lanky athlete tried not to let his nervousness show. He knew European history would be a tough class, but if he could pull off a decent grade, it would make it a lot easier to get accepted into a good college—he had Pepperdine University in his sights. With his backpack slung over his shoulder, Chad caught up with a couple of buddies who had also signed up for the class, and together they entered the classroom, which consisted mostly of old overstuffed couches along with a few desks. Hung on the walls were pictures—mostly of Mr. Corbett, including one of him wrestling a bear and another of him holding an assault rifle. The couches formed a semicircle directly in front of Mr. Corbett's desk and were full, so Chad grabbed a desk in back and took out a notebook as Mr. Corbett began talking.

"From the very first day when I heard him speak, I knew things were going to be a little different," Chad recalled. "And by the end of the first week of going to his class, I could see that he wasn't so much a teacher but a spokesman for his personal beliefs. It was really weird because he would assign us to read a bunch of chapters from the textbook every day, but when we got into his class all he talked about were his own beliefs—he never talked about the stuff he assigned us to read. But then the tests and quizzes he gave us were about the things in the textbook, so we basically had to teach ourselves."

Among the many things Mr. Corbett talked about, his favorite whipping boy appeared to be the very faith that had become increasingly important to Chad.

"On a daily basis he would bash Christianity. For example, he told us that if we looked at the world through 'Jesus glasses' it obscured the truth. Another one of his favorites was that believing in God was like believing in the spaghetti monster behind the moon. He also told us that Christians are more likely than other people to commit murder and rape. And this wasn't just something he did occasionally. He did it all the time."

His favorite whipping boy appeared to be the very faith that had become increasingly important to Chad.

Scattered within his rants against Christianity, Mr. Corbett would actually say a few things about the daily assignments. Chad noticed a friend taping the lectures, so he asked the student why he was doing that. His classmate said he wanted to make sure he didn't miss anything that actually applied to the textbook, and that made sense to Chad. He started bringing a small recorder to class with him, thinking this would help prepare him for those pop quizzes and unit tests.

"But when I would listen to the tapes at night, it just struck me that so much of what he did was say derogatory things about Christianity and conservative values. Since both were important to me, of course I was offended. It didn't seem fair that he could use his position as a teacher to ridicule my faith and values."

Chad wasn't the only student who found Mr. Corbett's attacks on Christianity offensive. By his reckoning, Chad thought about half the students thought it was wrong for a teacher to ridicule a person's beliefs. But the other half loved it, laughing at all of Mr. Corbett's sarcastic comments about Christians and conservative values. There were times that Chad wanted to challenge his teacher, but most of the time he felt helpless. He was fifteen years old, for crying out loud. Clearly Chad was no match for the imposing authoritative teacher.

"Not only was he older and significantly more intelligent than most high school sophomores, he could also be pretty intimidating. He wasn't a big guy, but he would sit up on this stool in front of the class to make him look bigger. Every now and then someone would try to argue with him, but he cut them down to size pretty quickly. And you wouldn't just be standing up to Mr. Corbett, but all those other students who thought he was such a cool teacher. It was a hostile environment for anyone who was a Christian or had conservative beliefs."

After a few weeks, several of Chad's friends dropped the class rather than tolerate Mr. Corbett's daily rants, but Chad was determined to stick it out.

"After every class I remember thinking, *Just drop the class. Drop the class and forget about it.* But something inside of me said, *No you can't. That's what everyone else has been doing for the last fifteen years.* I was planning on going to college and needed this class on my transcripts. But I didn't know what to do. I felt under a lot of pressure about the whole thing, so I talked with my mom and had her listen to one of the tapes."

The last thing any high-school guy wants is to have his mom show up at school to fight his battles. Thankfully Teresa was a wise woman and knew that as much as she wanted to go give Mr. Corbett a piece of her mind, this was Chad's battle. Through their church she had learned about an organization called Advocates for Faith and Freedom that focuses exclusively on protecting the religious freedom of individuals. She gave them a call, and when Chad came home from school the next day, he was a little surprised to see two lawyers sitting in his living room.

"Bof Tyler and Jennifer Bursch, lawyers for Advocates for Faith and Freedom, were great— they listened to me and after I explained what was going on at school they told me that my constitutional rights were being violated and that I could do something about it if I wanted to. That was really impor-

A verse that kept running through my mind: "I can do all things through Christ who strengthens me."

tant to me because up until then I thought I just either had to take it or quit. I was excited, but at the same time I wasn't sure if I could go against my school. I needed a couple of days to think and pray about it, and God seemed to be giving me a verse that kept running through my mind: 'I can do all things through Christ who strengthens me.'"

Chad also spent a lot of time talking with his parents, who assured him that whatever he chose to do they would stand with him. They never pressured him one way or the other, but let him know they would be there for him regardless. He decided the best way to handle the problem would be for him to seek a meeting with school officials to formally file a complaint against Mr. Corbett. When school officials refused to correct the situation, Chad knew what he had to do but had no idea the furor it would create.

"When we filed a lawsuit seeking the dismissal of Mr. Corbett for violating my First Amendment rights, things just exploded. I kept getting all these calls from the networks and other media asking me to do interviews. It really got bad after I appeared on Bill O'Reilly's program. It was pretty crazy."

It also was a little scary for Chad. Imagine walking through the halls of your high school when you're in the news every day. For suing your school and one of its coolest teachers. You walk past a group of students and hear the laughter, the insults. Some of your friends who believe the same way you do keep their distance because they don't want to be ridiculed or ostracized. Some teachers privately let you know they're pulling for you, but others glare at you in the name of academic freedom. *How can a religious fanatic like you think you can tell us what we can do in the classroom?*

"The hardest part for me was the reaction from my fellow students. The ones who supported me were far less vocal than those who were against me. In fact, they questioned why I was making such a big deal about it. The students supporting Mr. Corbett basically treated me like I was a jerk. They even organized this big rally against me. Not so much from my so-called supporters, and that really hurt. My principal seemed to be okay with me personally but was pretty upset with all the attention the lawsuit brought on to the school, especially the questions of why he let it get this far. For a long time I felt pretty alone."

Once the lawsuit was filed, it became clear that Chad couldn't stay in Mr. Corbett's class. At the same time, the school knew they had an obligation to find a way for him to get credit for the coveted class, so they arranged for him to continue taking European history as an independent study. In a way, he reasoned, that's what he and the rest of the students had to do anyway, since very little class time was spent on actual European history. So as the others met with Mr. Corbett to listen to his latest screed, Chad headed for the library where he studied the textbook, took the tests, and completed the other assignments.

"Every now and then I would see him in the hall, and he would give me dirty looks," Chad recalled, laughing.

But going to school every day when you're the center of a controversy is no laughing matter for an ordinary high-school student. The easy-going athlete began receiving threats, and bloggers around the nation were having a heyday at his expense. One wrote, "Chad Farnan is a self-righteously moronic creationist wanker who deserves to have his

The hardest part for me was the reaction from my fellow students.

stupidity pointed out publicly, in the classroom and out of it, far and wide. Spread the word." I guess inclusiveness is only offered to those who believe as you do. Sometimes the pressure and publicity seemed overwhelming, causing Chad to second-guess himself almost daily.

"I would love to say that my resolve was strong throughout all of this, but it wasn't. It was really hard. I remember thinking most of the time, *What have I done? This is insane. I can't handle this.* I felt really alone and wanted to call the whole thing off, but whenever I felt like giving up, I would read my Bible and pray, and it was like God was telling me that when you do the right thing, you will always face opposition, but He will always be there with me. That's what kept me going."

I'm always interested in the way Christians respond to challenges to their beliefs. For some, persecution and oppression strengthens their faith, while for others, it weakens their resolve to follow Christ. For every martyr, there are probably hundreds of Christians who try to blend into the crowd and not be recognized. Even Peter, a stalwart among the disciples, denied he even knew Jesus when it could have cost him his life. Which is why I appreciate Chad's honesty when I asked him how this experience affected his faith.

"At first, I'd have to admit my faith took a bit of a hit. I found myself questioning whether or not I had done the right thing. But in the long run, taking a stand really increased my faith, and I think a lot of that had to do with the foundation I had built. Back when I was in middle school, I was really a strong Christian. I read the Bible before I went to school and again at night. I prayed regularly and grew from the strong biblical teaching at my church. And though I wavered a little when this whole thing exploded, that foundation carried me to the point that I started to grow even deeper as a Christian and grow as a man too."

Chad also credits his church for walking through the fire with him.

"I got a lot of support from the pastors, but what really blew me away were the number of people from church I didn't even know who would come up to me and thank me for what I was doing and for being a good role model for their children. That had a huge impact on me and gave me the courage to continue."

In the long run, taking a stand really increased my faith.

When the district court ruled in Chad's favor, he felt exonerated. His critics had suggested all along that the case had no merit and that he was just doing this to get his fifteen minutes of fame—fame he never wanted. But his relief was short lived, as Mr. Corbett appealed the decision to the Ninth Circuit Court where the judge ruled in the teacher's favor on all but one count.

"Sure it was disappointing to lose, but all in all, I'm glad I took a stand, even if it was unpopular with so many people. It set a precedent and served notice to teachers that Christians are not going to tolerate efforts to discredit their faith and beliefs. They had never had a case like this, which is why I think they had such a hard time ruling on it. So even though we lost, I hope that there are other kids out there who will hear about my case and be willing to stand up for their faith too. If that happens, I will be even more grateful to have done what I did."

What I love about Chad is that he's a pretty ordinary guy who took an extraordinary stand for his faith. When he showed up with his friends to begin his sophomore year of high school, all he had on his mind were sports, hanging out with his friends, and getting good enough grades to get into college someday. He wasn't looking for a fight—certainly not a constitutional battle—nor did he think of himself as being especially courageous. But when it came time for him to act, he didn't hesitate.

> Increasingly, more and more ordinary people like Chad will be faced with the same decision.

Increasingly, more and more ordinary people like Chad will be faced with the same decision. Do I stand on the sidelines as my faith and values are threatened? Or do I stand up for what I believe, regardless of the cost? The Bible calls us to "put on the whole armor of God" (Ephesians 6:11) so that we can withstand the attacks of the Enemy. For Chad, he donned the armor when he decided to follow Christ at a young age and developed a subsequent hunger to grow in his newfound faith.

Chad survived not only the attacks on his faith, but he gained the ability to defend his Christian beliefs. He got into Pepperdine, the college of his choice, and graduated with a degree in business. He still loves sports, hanging out with friends, and living in Southern California. He doesn't think of himself as anything special—still pretty ordinary. Which is where most of us live. Until it's our time to stand. If Chad can do it, so can you.

> Blessed is the man who perseveres under trial, because when he has stood the test, he will receive the crown of life that God has promised to those who love him.
> (James 1:12, NIV)

■ ■ ■

Chad is not the first to be minding his own business, going about his activities only to find himself being called to lead. In the book of Judges, Gideon was once such an individual.

Israel was in bad shape. Their economy was in shambles. The people were in despair. They had entered this period of decline because they had lost their "fear" of God and began worshiping the gods of the Amorites in direct contradiction to God's instructions (Judges 6:10). As a result God had lifted His hand of protection, allowing the Midianites to terrorize the children of Israel.

Gideon was not looking to make a name for himself, nor had he applied to become a judge of Israel, which he did become. In fact, Gideon was still living at home with his parents. I doubt the reason was he was trying to pay off student loans! More likely—he was just trying to help his family survive.

When Gideon was tapped by God to stand up and defend the rights of his people, he was hunkered down in a winepress, threshing wheat. A winepress was carved out of the stone in the ground, which would have allowed him to conceal the wheat from the marauding Midianites. It was here that the Angel of the Lord, or the pre-incarnate Jesus Christ, appeared to him saying, "The LORD is with you, you mighty man of valor!" (verse 12).

I have to wonder what went through Gideon's mind at that moment. I am pretty confident that he did not see himself the same way God saw him. Gideon began a litany of reasons he was not the guy God was looking for: "O my Lord, how can I save Israel? Indeed my clan is the weakest in Manasseh, and I am the least in my father's house" (verse 15).

Gideon had not realized yet that he was talking to the Lord.

You hear in Gideon's words a sense of genuine humility, which is a common trait among those whom God is able to use to accomplish great things. There is also a very encouraging aspect to this exchange that the Lord has with Gideon. There is nothing to suggest that Gideon was super talented. No evidence that he was a great athlete or superior student. The words to Gideon reveal that God sees us for what we can be, not what we are!

Gideon had not realized yet that he was talking to the Lord. It wasn't until Gideon prepared and presented an offering, which was consumed by fire that arose out of the rock, that he understood he was talking to the Lord. At that point fear swept across him because he was face to face with God.

Why would he be fearful? Because the Lord is holy and we are not! When Isaiah saw a vision of the Lord at the time he was called to be a prophet, he said, "Woe is me, for I am undone! Because I am a man of unclean lips, and I dwell in the midst of a people of unclean lips; for my eyes have seen the King, the LORD of hosts" (Isaiah 6:5). We should never take lightly or casually God's call to serve Him.

The Lord reassured Gideon when He said, "Peace be with you; do not fear, you shall not die" (Judges 6:23).

Now that God had Gideon's undivided attention, He presented him with his first assignment. It was to destroy the town's sacred cow of sorts, a wooden image of Asherah, a Canaanite goddess, and the altar to Baal that went with it. He was then to slaughter one of his father's oxen, and using the wood from the image of Asherah, he was to present a burnt offering to the Lord.

God called Gideon to challenge that which was at the very heart of what ailed the nation—spiritual idolatry.

So how do you think his friends and neighbors responded? Do you think they celebrated his courage to stand up for the one true God as he tore down the false ones? Not exactly! Actually, they wanted to kill him (verse 30)!

The people were so spiritually blind that they wanted to kill the person who tore down the altar to the god of their enemies! Yes, they had allowed the worship of the true God to take a backseat to inanimate gods of the people who terrorized them. They were clueless!

An idol doesn't have to be constructed of wood or stone. In our lives, both individually and collectively as a society, an idol is something that takes the place of preeminence that rightfully belongs to God alone. It can be any number of things: entertainment, sports, money, sex, education, jobs, government, and the list goes on. With this understanding of what an idol can be, it explains the irrational and often hostile reactions of some when the veracity of these idols is challenged.

Notice only one person comes to Gideon's defense—his father. Joash wisely quiets the raging mob by laying out a very logical solution: if Baal is real, let him speak for himself by morning (verse 31). When the sun rose the next morning, Baal had not been heard from, so he obviously wasn't too upset about his altar being torn down. Having been delivered from the fear of his own people, Gideon was now prepared to move to the next challenge of leading his people against their oppressors.

MAKING IT REAL

1. Do you have a desire in your heart to serve the Lord, but you just don't see any opportunities? In reality, opportunities are all around us. God is looking for those—like Chad Farnan—who are responding to the needs at hand. Gideon was threshing wheat so his family could have bread to eat—what can be more basic than that? From that posture of humility and responsibility, God gave Gideon an opportunity. Be faithful in what God has given you to do; God will find you.

2. Maybe you see opportunity but don't feel qualified. You may wonder, *How in the world could God use me?* Remember, God sees you for what you can be when you are yielded to Him. It's good to know that in and of ourselves we can do nothing, but through Christ we can do all things.

3. Has God called you to take on the sacred cows of our day? Standing up for Jesus is taking on the false gods, because Jesus said, "I am the way, the truth, and the life. No one comes to the Father except through Me" (John 14:6). Be prepared for the hostility, the threats, and yes, the loss of friends that may come when God calls you to climb out of the winepress and stand up for Jesus. At those times of testing, pray and ask the Lord to give you the courage to stand and then listen for Him to speak the same words He spoke to Gideon: "The LORD is with you, you mighty man of valor!'" (Judges 6:12).

6

I Can Change Things

It was unusually warm for the last day of January, almost breaking the record for the highest temperature ever on what should have been another bone-chilling day in Baltimore, Maryland. But it wasn't the sultry weather that caused fourteen-year-old Sarah Crank's hands to perspire on that January afternoon in 2012.

One glance around the nicely appointed room, which spoke of important decisions and important people, was all it took to recognize that Sarah stood out in the Maryland State Senate hearing room. Normally the room would be full, but this was toward the end of the day and most of the spectators had left. So it was just Sarah and the twenty senators—most of whom were three and four times her age—and a handful of ordinary citizens. She could tell that the politicians were ready to call it a day, which was fine with her because that meant they probably wouldn't ask her a lot of questions. She just hoped they would listen and take her comments seriously.

Little did she know that what she was about to say would make her the target of unbelievably vile and vicious attacks.

Sarah Crank in many ways is a typical teenager. The blond-haired and sparkly blue-eyed girl likes to read, go shopping with her sister, post funny things on her Facebook page, rollerblade with her dad, and read the Bible with her close-knit family.

You read that right. A teenager who enjoys sitting in the living room with her mom and dad and little sister as they read the Bible together and then talk about what it all means.

"My dad always made it fun for us," she explained. "Like sometimes he would put one of our names in place of the actual name in a Bible verse, and that helped it make sense to us. It's just something we liked to do as a family and kept us close."

Sarah also likes pageants.

"When I was a little girl I didn't really think much about pageants. We don't have a TV so I never watched the show *Toddlers and Tiaras,* but I knew about Miss America and I guess I was really a 'girly girl' and liked the idea of dressing up in pretty dresses. So, when I first heard about the pageant in our city I was like 'Oh this sounds cool!' and after hesitating over whether I should try it, I finally entered my first pageant."

She quickly discovered that deciding to do something is the easy part. Following through with your good intentions takes commitment and courage.

"It was a lot of work to begin with because you've got to go out and find a sponsor and then do some fund-raising to pay for everything. But when I went to the first practice, everyone was really nice and one of my friends was doing it with me, which helped. And then on the night of the pageant I got really nervous about having to go up on stage in front of so many people. But overall, I had such a great time competing—it was really fun."

And a lot of hard work. The first time she competed in her

city's Junior Miss pageant, she finished "second alternate." She entered again the next year and once again claimed "second alternate."

As I said, Sarah is a very nice girl, but don't let that niceness fool you. She's also tough. Tenacious. Once she starts something, she has learned to finish it, regardless of the cost. For many people who enter a pageant and come in second two times in a row, they might think it's time to hang their gown in the closet and try something else. Not Sarah. After narrowly missing the crown twice, she had one more year of eligibility in the Junior Miss category.

> She quickly discovered that deciding to do something is the easy part. Following through with your good intentions takes commitment and courage.

She also had an important reason for wanting to win so badly.

"If you win, you would get a scholarship for college. I remember my mom telling me about college and how she had to work so hard to pay for it, so I knew if I wanted to go to college I'd have to start saving my money early, and winning the pageant would be a great way to start saving money for college."

So when it came time for her to hit the stage, a lot was on the line for Sarah.

Okay, this is it for me, she thought to herself. *It's my last chance, and I'm just going to give it my best shot and hope I win.*

And she did. Like a slugger at bat in the ninth inning with two outs and the count at three and two, Sarah hit a home run and grabbed the Junior Miss title.

"I was so excited, I actually started crying on stage because

I'd worked so hard for the past three years of the pageant, and I was just so thrilled that I had finally won!"

So how does a self-proclaimed girly-girl who likes to go shopping and hang out with her girlfriends end up on the receiving end of so much bullying and hate-filled threats? I mean, here's a girl who probably weighs eighty pounds soaking wet, has a smile that could melt titanium, and reads the Bible each day.

Actually, it's that last part that might be to blame, but I'm getting ahead of myself.

It turns out that Sarah's mother, Kathleen, had been following a troubling development in the Maryland State Senate. A bill was soon to be voted on that would redefine marriage from its historical and biblical definition of a man and woman to the joining of any two persons regardless of their gender. When hearings were scheduled in the judiciary committee, she decided that she couldn't just sit back and complain about the potential impact the redefinition of marriage would have on school curriculum or religious freedom; she had to do something. As with many state legislatures, anyone can testify for or against a measure in the state of Maryland, so she signed up.

Sarah was thrilled to learn that her mother would be testifying before the senate. Even though she was only fourteen years old, she followed the news enough to know that natural marriage was under attack, and it made her proud to think of her mom walking into the senate chambers to speak up for her beliefs and the beliefs of millions of other Americans. That is, until she learned that the day her mom was scheduled to appear before the judiciary committee was Sarah's birthday. Birthdays were a big deal in the Crank family, and though Sarah didn't want to get in the way of her mom's plans to testify, it just wouldn't be the same if she could not spend her birthday with her mother.

"But then I thought maybe I could go along with her and testify too. My mom had told me that the people in favor of same-sex marriage had kids go to the committee and testify, and that when kids testify it gets a lot of attention. So why couldn't I go and stand up for what *I* believe about marriage?"

Sarah's views on marriage were shaped not only by the example of a loving mother and father but by her Christian faith.

"I guess I'm a romantic, because even as a little girl I loved going to weddings and thought how neat it would be to find the right husband. So when I learned that people of the same gender wanted to get married, I just thought it was really bizarre, and I didn't like the idea of it because it went against what the Bible taught. Most of the people who testify before the senate are adults or professors who've done a lot of studies, but I felt my beliefs were just as important. When the day came to go before the senate, however, I was really nervous."

Why couldn't I go and stand up for what I believe about marriage?

Sarah and her mom arrived at the state capitol early in the day, but because they had signed up so late in the process, they had to wait all day in the stuffy chambers as, one by one, people testified either for or against the bill that was designed to redefine the six-thousand-year-old institution of marriage. Finally the moment came when the perky fourteen-year-old was called to the podium.

"I was so nervous that my hands were shaking, but I had

written out my testimony and I did my best to read it loud and clear so they knew exactly how I felt about the bill. It wasn't very long, and I don't remember everything I said, but I basically told them that if they passed the bill it would infringe on my beliefs about marriage as well as everyone else who believes marriage was never intended to be for people of the same gender. I also told them it was my fourteenth birthday and the best birthday present I could possibly wish for would be for them to vote no on gay marriage. By the time I was done, I was relieved to have it behind me, but I was also really glad I did it."

Since Sarah was one of the last to testify, the hearing adjourned shortly after she spoke; and as the legislators filed out of the hearing room, Sarah and her mom were milling about in the lobby when a man asked Sarah how to spell her name. It was then that she discovered someone had recorded her entire testimony with a video camera.

"When I realized that someone made a video of me, I thought it would be pretty cool to maybe someday see myself on television or something."

Little did she know that the video was made by an organization in favor of same-sex marriage, and it wouldn't be long before she discovered their *real* intentions. Within twenty-four hours, the video of her testimony was uploaded to YouTube, and that's when things started to get scary for Sarah.

"At first it was kinda neat because we would check every day to see how many people had seen the video. One day there were a hundred, and then ten thousand, and then seventy thousand! My parents wouldn't let me read the comments at first, so I just thought it was great that so many people heard me defend marriage."

But eventually her parents shared with her the nature of the comments posted on YouTube.

"My parents decided to tell me about all the bad comments so I could watch my back when I was out in the public. I didn't really read all the comments, but I knew there were death threats and a lot of really mean insults."

Full Text of Sarah's Testimony

Hi, I'm Sarah Crank. Today's my fourteenth birthday, and it would be the best birthday present ever if you would vote no on gay marriage. I really feel bad for the kids who have two parents of the same gender. Even though some kids think it's fine, they have no idea what kind of wonderful experiences they miss out on. I don't want more kids to get confused about what's right and okay. I really don't want to grow up in a world where marriage isn't such a special thing anymore.

It's rather scary to think that when I grow up the legislature or the court can change the definition of any word they want. If they could change the definition of marriage, then they could change the definition of any word. People have the choice to be gay, but I don't want to be affected by their choice. People say that they were born that way, but I've met really nice adults who did change. So please vote no on gay marriage. Thank you.

I've been targeted by a lot of anti-Christian groups like the Southern Poverty Law Center and the Human Rights Campaign, but I've never seen such vicious comments as the ones aimed at this fourteen-year-old girl. Like the one that spewed "If I ever see this girl, I will kill her. That's a promise." And that was far from the most offensive. It was an all-out vile attack on Sarah, her parents, and the Christian faith, all because a young teenage girl chose not what was most convenient or comfortable for her, but instead to stand for what she knew was best for her, her friends, and for her country.

As I said earlier, Sarah's tough. The attacks certainly got her attention, but she's not backing down. "If people think being mean to me is going to stop me, they're wrong. In fact, the way they have been so mean might actually get more people who are on the fence about this issue to consider my position, because who would want to join anyone who has to say such horrible things when their opinions are challenged?"

Despite all the publicity and attacks, Sarah Crank has managed to keep her smile and enjoy being a teenager. Rather than cause her to shrink back or hide her Christian beliefs, she's more determined than ever to stand up and speak the truth, speak it in love, but speak the truth nonetheless.

"This whole experience has really changed me. When I was younger the whole world was such a nice, happy place, but now I see that people can be rather ruthless and mean. The Bible teaches us to hate the sin but love the sinner, so I'm really sad for all those mean people because that can't be a good way to live. But if anything, this experience has made me more confident in myself and what I believe. Those people trying to bully me aren't going to stop me. They think I'll get scared and either keep

Even if I'm just a fourteen-year-old, I can stand up for what I believe. I can change things.

quiet or change my beliefs, but it's not working. Even if I'm just a fourteen-year-old, I can stand up for what I believe. I can change things."

...

And so I will go to the king, which is against the law; and if I perish, I perish! (Esther 4:16)

Did you know that there was actually a young girl in the Bible who also won a beauty pageant? It may have actually been the first recorded beauty pageant in history. She then risked her crown, along with her own life, to speak out—not for herself—but for the well-being of others. It is the account of a young Jewish orphan girl named Esther.

Esther, whose parents died when she was a child, was raised by her uncle Mordecai. They lived in Shushan, one of the main capitals of the Persian empire during the time of the Jewish Diaspora, roughly around 485 BC. The king at the time was Ahasuerus who, based upon the book of Esther, was in need of anger management.

Following a seven-day drinking feast, Ahasuerus summoned

his then queen, Vashti, to show off her beauty to his guests in the royal court. Apparently not interested in being a showpiece, Vashti refused, and he issued an irrevocable decree declaring her persona non grata in the royal court and sent copies of the decree throughout the empire. When he sobered up and cooled off, he realized he had messed up, as he missed the queen. The decrees of the Persian kings were irrevocable, so in an effort to appease Ahasuerus, his servants began organizing an official pageant of the most beautiful girls in the empire.

The Twitter version of the story is this: Esther wins Persian beauty pageant and is crowned queen of the world's largest empire. But this story is about much more than Miss Persian Empire; this is the story about the destiny of the Jewish people and the spiritual well-being of the entire world.

This was about four hundred and eighty years before the birth of Jesus Christ, and the king of the Persian empire had unwittingly issued an irrevocable decree that authorized the extermination of the Jewish people. Think about that for a moment.

No Jewish people, no Jesus!

But God, as He has from the beginning of time, uses ordinary people to accomplish extraordinary acts to bring about His plans and purposes, and this was Esther's time.

This story of Esther has relevance to us as it pertains to putting our fears aside and standing up for truth and righteousness. You may be thinking, *I am never going to be in a position to speak out and influence leaders like Esther did.* Not so fast!

Do you really think a teenage Esther said to herself, *I am going to influence the world's most powerful leader so that I can save the Jewish people!* I seriously doubt it! Esther was probably the most unlikely candidate for such a feat—at least in the eyes of the world. After all, she was an orphan, raised by her father's brother. Despite her uncle's devotion to her, I imagine that she may have been somewhat insecure and questioned whether or not she would have a future, let alone a future as a queen.

This brings us to the first aspect of Esther's life as it relates to each of us. If we will follow God and place Him at the center of our lives, He will place us in positions where our lives will have influence and eternal significance beyond what we could ever imagine. History is filled with ordinary men, women, boys, and girls like Esther and Sarah who were in just the right place, at just the right time, and they chose to stand and speak for truth and justice without compromise. But being in the right position is not enough; you have to be prepared.

> God, as He has from the beginning of time, uses ordinary people to accomplish extraordinary acts.

We now come back to the issue of fear. It is fear—fear of man, fear of failure, fear of rejection—that has kept more than a few from experiencing the significance that God has intended for them. You may recall the twelve spies who went into Canaan to scope out the promised land that God had given to them. Ten of the twelve came back and dissuaded the Israelites from going forward into the inheritance that God had promised to Abraham, which resulted in a forty-year road trip in the wilderness until that entire generation died off. Why? Because ten of those men, who were placed in positions to influence others, were gripped by the fear of man.

Uncle Mordecai informed Esther of the insidious decree orchestrated by a guy named Haman, the king's evil right-hand man who hated the Jews with a passion. Mordecai told Esther she was the only one who could get to the king in time to stop the pending extermination of the Jewish race, and the clock was ticking.

It was not as easy as it sounded. Esther faced fears similar to the spies'. While it sounds a bit crazy today, in Esther's day you didn't just walk into the king's office when you needed something. In fact, you couldn't even schedule an appointment with the king. A visit with the king was by invitation only, with one exception. But it was a risky exception.

A person could approach the inner court, and if the king extended the royal scepter, the person could enter. What's the risk? If the king did not extend the scepter, the person was executed. This applied to everyone, including the queen, of which Esther reminded Mordecai.

Mordecai's response to Esther's objections to taking the matter to the king was blunt. "Do not think in your heart that you will escape in the king's palace any more than all the other Jews. For if you remain completely silent at this time, relief and deliverance will arise for the Jews from another place, but you and your father's house will perish. Yet who knows whether you have come to the kingdom for such a time as this?" (Esther 4:13–14).

Convicted by the truth of her uncle's words, Esther embraced the antidote to fear. What's the antidote to fear, you ask? A humble declaration of our total and absolute dependence upon God!

Esther told Mordecai to "gather all the Jews . . . and fast for me; neither eat nor drink for three days, night or day. My maids and I will fast likewise. And so I will go to the king, which is against the law; and if I perish, I perish!" (verse 16).

Esther spiritually prepared for the challenge that was before her. An eternal perspective, which we gain through prayer and studying the Word of God, gives us the courage to overcome the temporal fears we face in this life. For Esther, it came down to this: the worst that could happen was that she could die, so if she died, she died.

> The antidote to fear: a humble declaration of our total and absolute dependence upon God!

Jesus encouraged this view in Matthew 10:28 where He said, "Do not fear those who kill the body but cannot kill the soul. But rather fear Him who is able to destroy both soul and body in hell." In other words, our reverence for God should eclipse any fear we have of man.

Prayer was the beginning of Esther's preparation, and so it should be with us. But it does not stop there. Whether Esther's plan of how to approach the king was revealed to her as the result of her praying and fasting we don't know. But we do know that she used wisdom in appealing to the king. We too must use wisdom and make the necessary preparations as we are positioned to influence leaders and others.

MAKING IT REAL

1. In a world with a population of seven billion people, which often seems controlled by a handful of the wealthy and powerful, it is tempting to think that God could never use us to make a difference, much as Sarah Crank once believed. We don't have to look far to find someone who is wealthier, better educated, or from a more influential

family. But those things, as we see from the life of Esther, do not limit what God can do through our lives. Have you asked the Lord to use you? Have you said, "Here am I! Send me" (Isaiah 6:8)?

2. Are you preparing to face the challenges that will certainly come your way as God positions you to influence others? How's your prayer life? Are you spending time meditating upon God's Word? Read Psalm 1.

3. Take a few minutes and think about this: Have you come to a point in your relationship with God that it means more than anything else to you? Are you willing to risk it all to obey God and serve Him? Can you say like Esther, "If I perish, I perish!"?

7

You Don't Have to Be Perfect

Ryan Bomberger shouldn't be here. Ryan's biological mother was raped. Conventional thinking, even among some Christians, is that if a woman is raped and conceives a child from that rape, abortion is morally justified and culturally encouraged. Ryan was the baby conceived by that rape, and most would have expected the woman carrying him in her womb to end his life. Better for her, since the child would have been a constant reminder of her trauma. Better for him, since he was not an eagerly awaited, planned addition to a family and would likely be abused or neglected or another burden on society. Better for all of us to just look the other way as this woman quietly walked to the clinic to deal with this horrible tragedy.

"Yes," we might say, "abortion is wrong, but how can we force a woman to carry a child conceived in such a violent, demeaning manner?"

Ryan had no voice in the matter, but if he had, I suspect he would have wanted a chance to live.

Fortunately, he got that chance because his biological mother did not buy into that tidy little argument condoning abortion.

She courageously chose to carry her child, which ultimately led to his being adopted into a loving, multiracial family where ten of his twelve siblings were also adopted. It also led to Ryan's strong commitment to life. Strong enough to get him in trouble.

Ryan's biological mother had grown up under difficult circumstances, was a foster child, and eventually for unknown reasons became estranged from her foster parents. Once she was old enough, she joined the army, and it was while she was in the army that she was raped. She was white, her rapist black. The year was 1970, one year after another woman by the name of Norma Jean McCorvey discovered she was pregnant. Friends advised McCorvey to report falsely that she had been raped, because in Texas, where she lived, abortion was legal in the cases of rape or incest. Since she could not produce a police report of the "rape," she was unable to legally terminate her unwanted pregnancy. She then went to an illegal "backroom abortion clinic" only to discover authorities had already shut it down. So she hired two attorneys who took her case all the way to the Supreme Court, which ruled on January 22, 1973, that abortion was a fundamental right under the US Constitution. Norma Jean McCorvey was the Jane Roe in the infamous *Roe v. Wade* case that made abortion legal in the United States.

At the time, women serving in the armed forces were allowed to have abortions if they were raped. For whatever reason, Ryan's biological mom chose to keep the child instead. In fact, even as she carried Ryan in her womb, she made arrangements for him to be adopted.

"I like to think someone—a friend or family member— encouraged her to keep her child," Ryan told me. "Obviously, the fact that she could have aborted me played a huge role in my own pro-life beliefs."

Ryan, who describes himself as black and white, was given not only the gift of life by his biological mom, but the gift of godly parents—Henry and Andrea Bomberger—and three siblings. Ryan was their first adoption, but far from their last. Eventually, Henry and Andrea adopted nine more children from a variety of racial and ethnic backgrounds.

"I grew up with parents who loved the kids who were supposedly unlovable. Kids like me whose parents couldn't care for them. Kids with disabilities. And kids who definitely didn't look like the rest of the kids in the neighborhood. When they adopted me, they had to face a lot of unexpected, covert racism and even resistance from some extended family members. They weren't trying to make a statement or push an agenda. They just wanted to love kids that the world said would be unwanted. And that's exactly what they did."

> **I grew up with parents who loved the kids who were supposedly unlovable.**

One of Ryan's favorite memories was the family's annual vacation to the ocean. "Our folks would pile us all into this big van that was actually called a maxi-van," Ryan laughed as he recounted those trips.

"It was huge—it had to be to fit us all inside. We were jammed in there in those hot vinyl seats and no air conditioning. Since there was no room for the luggage, my dad pulled a camper behind the van with our suitcases stuffed into it. I absolutely loved those vacations, but what I remember most was that we definitely stood out. We didn't quite look like anyone else. It reminded me how close we were as a family—how much we loved being together. The world could look at us differently, but we didn't care."

For the Bombergers, togetherness was a way of life. When their family grew to eight, they moved into an old farmhouse in Lancaster, Pennsylvania. Three bedrooms for eight people seemed adequate at the time, but as they added more children to their family, they added on to the house. The children also helped out doing farm chores, an activity that ultimately may have contributed to a cap on the size of their family at thirteen.

"Mom and Dad wanted to adopt more kids, but the local social services agency suspected that they were exploiting us as child labor," Ryan explained with a grin. "Probably a social worker drove by when we were pulling weeds in the garden and said, 'That's it for them.'"

The eleven-acre farm was more of a hobby than anything, though because Henry's income wasn't enough to cover the family's expenses, he sold some of what they raised on the farm to make up the difference.

"We had cows, pigs, sheep, horses, and as a kid I always thought it was because they loved having lots of animals around, oblivious to the fact that they sold the wool from the sheep and meat from the cows and pigs. To us, it was just fun."

It was also a way to teach the kids responsibility. There were no freeloaders in the Bomberger family. At first, the girls did the inside work while the boys handled the outside chores. That all changed one day when Andrea decided the boys needed to learn to fold laundry, wash the dishes, and clean the bathrooms, and that the girls were fully capable of handling the outside work.

"My primary job became cleaning the bathrooms, and I

hated it. Getting down on my hands and knees, scrubbing around and on the toilet—not something anyone enjoys doing, but it taught me humility. And getting all of us involved in the work on the farm gave us a strong work ethic."

In addition to helping their parents on the farm, Ryan and his siblings attended both public and private schools; and they were all active in sports, music, and other extracurricular activities. On top of all that, their dad owned the local department store, and each took their turn helping out with a variety of tasks.

The social worker might call that child labor—I call it great parenting.

"I remember at age seven or eight sweeping out the store for twenty-five cents an hour and bagging ice for a nickel a bag."

The social worker might call that child labor—I call it great parenting. What a gift Ryan's parents gave their children, but as Ryan reminded me several times, most of the virtues and qualities they learned from their parents were not so much taught as caught. They demonstrated their beliefs by the way they lived, and perhaps the greatest lesson Ryan learned from them was that every life is important.

Growing up in a Christian home, Ryan made a decision to follow Christ when he was seven years old at his church's Vacation Bible School.

"But I really came to understand Christ's sacrifice for me when I was thirteen and attending a youth camp in the Poconos. Even though my parents always made me feel loved and valued, I struggled with a lot of issues, including a low self-esteem. To be honest, I was angry at God and really didn't believe He loved me. Our speaker was a woman—a missionary from Eastern Europe, and as she talked to us about how much God loved us, I sort of issued a challenge to God: 'If You really love me, have her come to me and tell me to my face that You love me.' As soon as I said that, I felt a hand on my shoulder. It was the missionary and she said to me, 'Are you ready now to believe God loves you?' From that moment on, everything changed for me."

It was also at that same time that Ryan fully understood the circumstances of his conception and birth, and initially he was devastated. But the more he thought about it, the more he began to see how incredible his birth mother's choice for life was. So for one of his assignments in the eighth grade, he prepared a speech about abortion, and in that speech he shared his own story with his classmates.

"Kids were crying, as I think for the first time in their young lives they understood what abortion really was," Ryan explained. "I realized that I have a story to tell, and from that moment on, helping others see that every life has value has been a passion of mine."

> From that moment on, helping others see that every life has value has been a passion of mine.

Even though the ensuing years presented some major challenges, that speech of a thirteen-year-old was a defining moment for Ryan. It planted a seed inside that would later blossom into something both remarkable and daunting.

In college and graduate school, Ryan was literally Big Man on Campus. Popular, a great student, volunteer youth mentor. A songwriter and vocalist, he was the lead singer for a band that was on the verge of signing a record deal. To pay for living expenses not covered by the full ride he received for his undergrad and graduate work, he deejayed at large-scale events, weddings, and parties. But on the inside he was empty—struggling to accept himself.

"I didn't realize it at the time, but my striving to be the best at everything was really an attempt to escape the intense self-loathing and self-rejection, which I firmly believe was largely a result of my biological mother's rejection of me," Ryan explained. "Science shows how an unborn baby is impacted by the emotions its mother experiences, and I know she must have been burdened with a lot of understandable anger and pain from being raped. Then there was the whole racial identity crisis that began in college. I often felt like I wasn't white enough or black enough. As if I didn't have a hard enough time accepting who I was, I allowed myself to be caught up in the destructive lie that I could be defined by my pigmentation. My faith was frayed, and I was just barely hanging on. With few exceptions, everyone around me thought I was living a charmed life.

> I experienced a spiritual deliverance that can only be described as coming from God.

"One night I was driving home from work, singing along to the Cindy Morgan song 'I Will Be Free,' a song I'd heard hundreds of times before. I'd made that drive dozens of times, always feeling so down about who I was deep inside. There were times that I just wanted to keep driving, but on this particular night, I can't even begin to explain what happened in my car. As I sang along with that song, I experienced a spiritual deliverance that can only be described as coming from God. We had this old trampoline in the backyard, and when I got home, I started jumping and singing and laughing and crying—I was just so happy for the deliverance from this struggle over the way my life started. And I've been free of those feelings ever since."

It wasn't long after this event that Ryan met his future wife, Bethany, at Regent University. Bold, creative, and fun-loving, Bethany is equally as passionate about her love for God. She had taught for ten years in inner-city schools and private suburban schools. Ryan worked for years as a creative director doing media production and developing ad campaigns. Once they got married, they both felt their hearts being pulled toward doing something that would make a greater difference in the lives of others.

"We both wanted more. We wanted to use the gifts God gave us to impact people, and the more we talked about that hunger in our lives, the more we began to see a clear picture of what God was calling us to do."

Earlier, Ryan had spoken at an event in Washington, DC, known simply as TheCall. Founded by Lou Engle in the spirit of Joel 2, it is a massive gathering of Christians praying and fasting and worshiping for spiritual renewal. After Ryan shared his story, it took him three hours to exit the stage area because so many people wanted to talk with him and share their own stories.

That was a pivotal event for Ryan—what he calls a divine download. As he and Bethany sought God's direction many years later, the spirit of that event could not be ignored. In a moment of great clarity, Bethany began sketching out their thinking on a notepad, and just like that, they launched the Radiance Foundation. Their mission: helping people understand and embrace their intrinsic value and live lives of meaning. Sort of what Ryan had been able to do, thanks to his biological mother, his adoptive parents, and a lot of support along the way. Between his creative skills and Bethany's educator's savvy, they would use various media to affirm the value of life.

For their maiden project, they created the first pro-adoption-themed ad campaign to address the disproportionate impact of abortion in the black community. According to Ryan, African Americans are up to five times more in danger of death by abortion than any other demographic. The campaign (www.toomany aborted.com) initially placed eighty billboards in and around Atlanta raising awareness of this fact, and "it was as if the Civil War had broken out," to put it in Ryan's words.

"Ironically, the NAACP denounced us over our second billboard campaign in Atlanta (called our Juneteenth Campaign), which simply declared, 'The 13th amendment freed us, abortion enslaves us—toomanyaborted.com.' The same thing happened in Oakland, California, where our billboards proclaimed 'Black is Beautiful—toomanyaborted.com.' The NAACP accused us of racism, saying that we gave the false impression that Planned Parenthood kills black babies."

In response, Ryan wrote an article for LifeNews.com, using the NAACP's own documents, their website, and their official resolution in 2004 affirming a woman's right to choose abortion—the first time they took a position affirming abortion "rights." The article detailed their pro-abortion actions, using a parody of the NAACP's name instead of their real name. Yet the NAACP responded with strong-arm cease-and-desist tactics, trying to get Ryan to pull the article from LifeNews.com and the Radiance Foundation's website.

Ryan refused to back down.

"We filed a declaratory action, fully expecting the judge to see this as a free-speech issue," Ryan recounted. "Not only was I protected by the Constitution to make fun of their name, but everything I wrote about them was true and based on their own publicly stated positions on abortion."

Ryan saw firsthand how twisted justice is in our morally relativistic culture. The case was tried in a three-day circus trial in the US District Court in Norfolk, Virginia. Judge Raymond Jackson heard all the evidence and then wrote a fifty-two-page decision basically saying that the NAACP had never taken a position on abortion. He went on to say that the NAACP had gone to great lengths to avoid taking a position on abortion, largely because so many clergy belong to the organization. Apparently the judge was unaware that Dr. William Barber, a clergyman and NAACP board member, recently had been given Planned Parenthood's inaugural "Care. No Matter What." Award. The judge also ruled that Ryan would have to erase anything written about the NAACP from Radiance's website, banned him from using the parodied name, and banned him from creating a new parody.

Still, Ryan wasn't giving up and has since appealed the case to the Fourth Circuit Court of Appeals.

"This is not just a pro-life issue. It's a free speech issue and an alarming example of a million-dollar organization using trademark law to censor speech it doesn't like—truth. I wasn't about to be shut up or silenced, which is why we're pursuing this."

The Goliath-like NAACP spent more than seven hundred thousand dollars fighting Ryan and even tried to get the judge to make Ryan and Radiance cover their costs. Fortunately, the judge ruled that Ryan would only have to pay seven thousand dollars, which in itself seems like a miscarriage of justice because all he did was expose the truth about an organization whose actions and words condoned abortion.

"Even paying one dollar for this would be egregious," Ryan emphasized. "So obviously we're fighting that as well, not because of the money but because of the principle of free speech."

At the time, Ryan and Bethany ran the Radiance Foundation out of a small office in their home. They knew the NAACP had limitless resources to fund this battle, yet never once did they consider backing down.

"Knowing what so many other pro-life people have gone through, I'd have to say I wasn't really surprised," he explained. "I guess I was dismayed more than anything because as a black (biracial) person, this was an organization I had once respected in my youth. Now they were going after me because I dared to call them out. I never thought I would be attacked by an organization that once defended the most vulnerable and disenfranchised."

I wasn't about to be shut up or silenced.

So how would you respond if a major advocacy organization spent hundreds of thousands of dollars trying to silence you because you dared to challenge their hypocrisy? Trust me, legal battles are not only expensive, but they can be daunting. In fact, many well-funded individuals and organizations quickly settle out of court when they are challenged, even if they know they are right. They just don't want to go through the trouble of fighting for their beliefs in a courtroom. Which is why I love Ryan's response when this all started.

"I was sitting at my desk in our home office when my wife ran in and asked, 'Did you get the e-mail?' The NAACP had e-mailed me with an attachment from their lawyer threatening to sue us. I looked up at my wife and my first response was 'Awesome!' God was giving me an opportunity to take a stand for life by showing what had become of a once-great organization that fought for the rights of black Americans."

Yes, according to today's standards, Ryan shouldn't be here. But I'm glad he is. His life is a shining example of the cause he and Bethany are devoted to: every person has value and can live a life of meaning. He could have backed down when he got that e-mail. Moved on to another project. Let someone else fight that battle. But he didn't—not because of politics or even the Constitution. He's fighting for a higher, nobler reason.

Every person has value and can live a life of meaning.

"There has to be a standard for any belief that we hold, and for me, that's God's Word. You simply cannot support abortion if you believe the Bible to be true. I know there are consequences when you engage in a fight like this. But there are bigger consequences for doing nothing."

■ ■ ■

If you think your past is an obstacle to living a life of meaning and being used by God, think again. One of the greatest leaders in the Bible was one of the most unlikely based upon his past. To say that Moses had some issues to overcome would be an understatement.

For starters, while he did have a mother who loved him and gave him life, she was forced to give up this Hebrew boy to be adopted and raised by an Egyptian in the cultural ways of the Egyptians. Additionally, he had a serious early midlife crisis at about forty years old when he killed an Egyptian whom he saw beating a Hebrew slave (Exodus 2:11–12). The crisis came when Pharaoh found out about the murder and sought to execute Moses, resulting in him fleeing to the backside of the desert.

Was Moses running from his past? Simple answer, yes!

He had settled into what he thought was his future as a shepherd. He found himself a good woman, probably had himself a one-eyed dog, a nice tent, a good ride (camel). He listened to a little country-western music, and beyond that he had no vision or plans for his life. Then he had an encounter with God.

Who knows what was on Moses's mind as he was looking after his father-in-law's sheep in the desert, when all of

When God calls and we answer, the journey has begun whether we are ready or not!

a sudden he stumbled upon a flaming bush. I doubt he was thinking about an encounter with God. But that is exactly what happened: God called his name from the center of the burning bush (Exodus 3:4), and Moses answered, "Here I am." At this point his whole life changed.

When God calls and we answer, the journey has begun whether we are ready or not!

God resolved that issue only for Moses to raise another. "When I come to the children of Israel and say to them, 'The God of your fathers has sent me to you,' and they say to me, 'What is His name?' what shall I say to them?" (verse 13).

God had an answer for that one too. "I AM WHO I AM" (verse 14). "But suppose they will not believe me or listen to my voice; suppose they say, 'The LORD has not appeared to you,'" Moses said (Exodus 4:1). As soon as God dealt with that concern, Moses basically said, "I can't talk very well" (verse 10).

God is patient and long-suffering, but there comes a point

when He gets tired of all our excuses, because it is ultimately not about us and what we can do; it's about God and what He can and will do when we obey Him.

While Moses clearly went too far in resisting God's call, there is merit in Moses's reluctance to enter the fray with Pharaoh. Moses was not a revolutionary looking for a fight with the political power broker of his day. It had to be absolutely clear that this was not about Moses wanting to settle an old score or make a name for himself. This was about God and His people. Likewise, while we don't want to resist God's call, we need to know, as Moses did, as Ryan did, that it was God who called.

Here is one way to determine our motivation. Are we taking a stand for God because we love the thrill of a fight or enjoy the intensity of conflict, or do we endure the conflict because we love the Lord? If we ever come to the point where we thrive on being in conflict with the world, it is time for a motives check.

What was the key to Moses's success as a leader? It was the intensity of his relationship with God. No other leader in the Bible spent more time with God and was as familiar with Him. In fact God spoke to Moses "as a man speaks to his friend" (Exodus 33:11). But that intimacy didn't just happen; it developed as Moses was repeatedly required to stand alone.

When you go toe to toe with power brokers like the pharaoh or the NAACP, you find out quickly just how hard standing up really is! Moses and Aaron had met with the elders of the children of Israel and told them what God had called them to do, and everyone was on board (Exodus 4:29–31). That is, until the first encounter with the pharaoh.

Like any major undertaking, the excitement quickly dissipated when things did not go as planned. Instead of responding to Moses's message from God to "let My people go," Pharaoh said, "Who is the LORD, that I should obey His voice?" Then to prove his point, he made life harder for the children of Israel by having them make bricks without providing the straw and beating them when they didn't make their quota (Exodus 5:1–2, 6–14). It didn't take long for the children of Israel to question the veracity of Moses and his mission.

This pattern was repeated over and over. Pharaoh's "hardened" heart was just as much about teaching Moses to stand in the face of unrelenting opposition as it was revealing the power of God.

As we saw with Moses, when things were going well, the people hailed him as a great leader and listened to him, but as soon as things didn't go as planned, Moses had to stand practically alone (Number 12:1). But Moses, being a man of great humility (verse 3), turned to God and not on the people. In fact, on more than one occasion Moses interceded with God on behalf of the rebellious people, asking God to spare their lives (Exodus 32:11; Numbers 12:13; 14:12–20; 16:22, 48; 21:7).

Because of his intimacy with God, Moses could face an oppressive and arrogant ruler and endure the resistance and rejection of the very people he was called to help.

MAKING IT REAL

1. No matter what your past, how you were conceived, what choices you made or even choices made for you, God wants a relationship with you. Like Moses, or like Ryan Bomberger, you can live a life of meaning, but it starts

with a life-altering encounter with God. Have you had that kind of encounter with God?

2. What is God's plan for your life? God has a mission for your life (Psalm 37:23). If you're not sure what God wants you to do with your life, ask Him and then listen!

3. Once you begin to hear the inner voice of the Holy Spirit speaking to you, take one sheet of paper, set the timer on your smartphone for ninety seconds, and write down what you believe God wants you to do with your life. Continue to pray over this plan, and then seek counsel from a spiritually mature Christian.

4. Know that to successfully stand for God, you have to spend time with God. How's your prayer life? Do you have a daily time of prayer and Bible study?

8

Flipping Houses, Not Convictions

Jason and David Benham are preacher's kids, and we all know what that means, right? Then when I tell you that they are also identical twins, you likely have this diabolical interest to hear about all the trouble they got themselves into. Which, of course, they did.

Like the time they discovered a bag of cement in a neighbor's garage and tried using it as hair gel on each other. Or their short-lived pastime of lofting rocks in the air at just the right trajectory so that they would come crashing down on the roof of a passing motorist's car. I'm sure there were more stories like this, but they shared another story with me that explains a lot about these two brothers. It occurred in the 1990s when their dad joined hundreds of others to silently protest in front of abortion clinics. Or as Jason explained, his dad preferred to call it "proclaiming the gospel at the mission field of an abortion clinic."

"I remember one time watching my dad praying at a clinic near our home in Dallas," David recounted. "He had already explained to us that he did this to try and save the lives of babies, and that had a real impact on me. But that day there was a lot of commotion, with a line of police on horseback patrolling the area.

I watched my dad go down, blood covering his face. That image burned in my heart. As I saw my dad stand bravely against the attack, I prayed, *God, I wanna be just like him!*"

David and Jason's father was a firm believer in the kind of discipline that focused less on punishment and more on lifestyle. In other words, the way to keep the twins in line was to keep them busy, which for him meant exercise. And lots of it. Up at six in the morning to run, do push-ups, and end with sit-ups. By the time they were in middle school he added a new feature to their daily workouts: push the family Volkswagen Beetle up and down their street.

It wasn't just the physical discipline their father introduced, but a shining example of how being a Christian is more than saying a prayer to accept God's free gift of salvation.

"Dad didn't just make us run—he modeled physical discipline himself, but with an added twist," Jason explained. "As he ran through the city, whoever he met he would shout out, 'Jesus loves you.' He would also stop to pick up trash, often returning home from his run with two bags of garbage. He believed that whatever you did, you should do it to the glory of God, and that's a lesson that rubbed off on us pretty strong."

Of course, the twins had other reasons for following their dad's disciplinary regimen. Both natural athletes, they dreamed of one day making it into the big leagues. Professional baseball. The burn in their legs from pushing that car, running through the neighborhood when both the temperature and humidity hovered around ninety-five, rolling out of bed to exercise when their buddies snoozed for another hour—all that sacrifice became the fuel for their dream. But it did something else. It slowly instilled in them a tenacity to persevere no matter what.

Which is a good thing, because as even the most talented superstar will tell you, the road to success in professional sports is rockier than a mountain-bike course. Despite the boys' leading their high-school baseball team in about every category, the much-hoped-for scholarships from the major universities— the ones who sent players on to the big leagues—never materialized. By this time, they had learned from both parents that God opens and closes doors for a reason.

He believed that whatever you did, you should do it to the glory of God.

So they prayed for God to help them understand why their baseball careers appeared to be stalled, only to be contacted a few days later by the baseball coach from Liberty University who wanted to visit the twins in their home and watch them play the next day. It turned out that the coach knew the boys had what it took to make the team at Liberty, he was more interested in their character. All that spiritual and physical discipline from Dad paid off, both boys were offered full rides to Liberty.

Their years at Liberty, where then chancellor and television pastor Dr. Jerry Falwell sat behind the dugout for each game, saw the twins grow on the field as well as off. By the time they graduated, both had landed contracts and were off to the next level—playing for farm teams affiliated with major league baseball. And here's where the story takes a divine left—or maybe right—turn. Blame it on injuries. Blame it on the stiff competition to make it to the next level. Or credit God for once again having bigger and better plans for Jason and David, like working as a janitor and answering phones at a call center.

"Sometimes God has to break us in order to use us for His

kingdom," David explained. "I was feeling sorry for myself because all I had ever dreamed of was playing professional baseball, and there I was with a broom in my hand. I remember crying out to Him and hearing His answer: *Be faithful right where I put you. Stop worrying about where you thought I was going to get you. You've made that an idol in your life. Just be faithful to Me.*"

Almost as a lark, they both got real-estate licenses and signed on with a respected firm, but their salaries were 100 percent commission based. So until they could sell a house and make some money, they began taking odd jobs, approaching menial tasks with the same dedication they applied to their dream of the big leagues. Word spread, which led to more jobs, and it was in this "putting food on the table" valley that they discovered they possessed an entrepreneurial talent. Specifically, the skill of buying older run-down houses, fixing them up, and then selling them for a profit—"flipping" as it's called.

> Sometimes God has to break us in order to use us for His kingdom.

It turns out they were pretty good flippers. Actually very good. After just a few years, they went from selling that first house to flipping six thousand for themselves and other clients. And that's where their story gets interesting. Benham Real Estate Group began attracting attention. The *Wall Street Journal* featured them. *Inc.* magazine named them "fastest growing private company." *Entrepreneur* magazine awarded them "Top New Franchise." Ernst & Young made them finalists in their "Entrepreneur of the Year" competition.

They began traveling the country, as demand for their speaking and consulting services skyrocketed. Whenever they had the opportunity to share their business principles, they always gave credit to God and the principles they learned from the Bible. The irony was not lost on them.

"We thought we were going to use the platform of baseball as a ministry, but God had switched that to the platform of business," David told me. "We now saw our business as our calling. God took one dream and turned it into something bigger and better for His glory."

As their company grew, they felt led to form companies that provided funding for missionaries in the Philippines. They called it "missioneering," and within a short time they provided work for 500 employees, with 250 of them praying to receive Christ through the influence of this endeavor. Their "missioneers" used the profits from their companies to start a sports league, a feeding program for 120 kids living in poverty, evangelism initiatives, and disaster-relief projects. The twins also launched two fitness centers they named "CrossFit," where their fitness instructors teach that "physical training is of *some* value, but godliness has value for all things" (1 Timothy 4:8, NIV, emphasis added).

Life was about as good as it gets for Jason and David. They had built an extremely successful business on biblical principles. They used their platform to share their love for God with others. They plowed their company's profits into ministries that gave people jobs and the gospel.

And then Dad called.

Now earlier I gave you a little information about Dad, but not the whole story. Especially not about his jail time. You see, when Dad gave his heart to Jesus as an adult, he went all in. Gave not only his heart but his whole life. He believed you not only profess your faith in Christ, but you live it. Every day. He called it "theology as biography." And when you see things that conflict with your faith, you don't close your eyes to it. If people are hungry, you feed them. If they are cold, you give them a coat. Because Jesus commands all of us to do these things.

And if a doctor performed abortions at a clinic, even though it was legal according to the laws of the land, it was wrong in the eyes of Jesus. So as a follower of that Jesus, you did what you could to stop the killing of innocent babies, even if it meant getting beat up. Or worse. In the early days of the pro-life movement, activists paid little attention to laws prohibiting them from protesting in front of abortion clinics, which led to a lot of protesters going to jail.

It was not unusual for Jason and David to come home from school and ask, "Where's Dad?" only to hear Mom casually reply, "He's in jail again."

If the Benham brothers thought Dad had mellowed over the years, his phone call put that notion to rest. The boys were in Utah at a job site; Dad was calling from Charlotte, North Carolina, where they all lived, calling to tell them it was just announced that the 2012 Democratic National Convention would be held in Charlotte.

"We've gotta show up!" he exclaimed into the phone. "I'm not sure what we'll do, but we've got to show up."

The brothers knew their dad well enough to know what he was thinking: *Whenever there was a large crowd of people—especially one that would receive national attention—Christians needed to be present as salt and light.* Jason and David shared their dad's belief that if God had allowed their city to host an event that the whole world would watch, it must be for a reason.

They also agreed that the nation had been slipping into moral decline, so this could be an opportunity to take a stand for biblical values.

At the same time, they wondered how taking such a stand might affect their rapidly growing business. After praying about it, they knew they had to obey God, but how? The more they thought about it, the more they realized that the responsibility for America's decline lay with the church, and the best thing they could do during the convention was to gather to repent and pray. That was it. Nothing political or sectarian. Just a public gathering to repent and pray for our nation. Less than 25 percent of Charlotte's churches participated—some of the megachurch pastors apparently felt that joining in might hurt their book sales.

> After praying about it, they knew they had to obey God.

Dad might have had a crazy idea, but on the night before the Democratic National Convention opened, more than nine thousand people from one hundred fifty churches showed up to acknowledge that America's decline points right back to the church. It was one of the most marvelous demonstrations of Christian unity ever, all because Dad listened to that still, small voice inside of him that said *Obey Me* and nudged us in the right direction to pull it off.

Over the years I've learned that it's when you're at the top of your game that the Enemy tries knocking you down. Jason and David were clearly at the top of their game. Their work and ministry were wonderfully aligned. Their business provided them with financial security. They had successfully led a city-wide effort that modeled Christian engagement in the broader world.

They were young, handsome, and energetic—the very stuff of television, which was their next opportunity.

Representatives from a television production company contacted the brothers to see if they might be interested in hosting a reality show. At first they were reluctant, but the production folks persisted, convincing them to at least shoot a "sizzle."

"We had no idea what a sizzle was, other than waking up to Mom cooking bacon," Jason laughed. "Turns out a sizzle was a short video designed to pitch to all the network executives in hopes of landing a deal. So we shot the sizzle and within a few days we had offers from five networks!"

Eventually they accepted a generous offer from Home and Garden Television (HGTV): a multi-year contract with the first cycle of six one-hour episodes guaranteed. According to the production team, this sort of deal was unheard of. Usually new television shows begin with a pilot—a single episode to test the response. If the pilot comes through, they then commit to a series. If the pilot flops, the show is over.

"We were feeling pretty good about ourselves when strange things began to happen," David recalled.

Strange indeed. As negotiations continued, the brothers got a phone call from their production company asking them if they were anti-gay.

"We were really taken off guard, but explained that we weren't anti-anything, but simply pro-family guys who believe the Bible and believe that marriage is between a man and a woman," Jason told me. But a website called Right Wing Watch wrote an article where they took the brothers' comments out of context to make it look like they hated gays. Something Right Wing Watch is notorious for doing.

Everything went silent. They heard nothing from HGTV or the production company, so the brothers thought it was over. They were so disappointed that they considered trying to cultivate a more positive image of Christians for the media, something that always sounds reasonable, but consistently fails. As their dad explained to them, they had to be who they were, and any attempt to hold back their beliefs would be a disservice to the kingdom. As I've seen over and over again, whenever Christians compromise or hide their faith in Jesus to try and fit in, they ultimately lose their power to influence the world for Christ. It was a tough lesson for the brothers, but they eventually accepted the loss of this reality program as the price for being true to God.

We were feeling pretty good about ourselves when strange things began to happen.

Then out of the blue, they got a call from a representative of HGTV inviting them to meet with him in Nashville. Since they had business in Nashville anyway, Jason and David thought, *What have we got to lose?* They agreed to meet for dinner at a local restaurant, and after they walked into the restaurant and sat down, their HGTV host shocked them.

"Are you guys going to sign with us or not?"

"We couldn't believe our ears," Jason recounted. "We thought the deal had gone down the tubes and had already accepted that. Apparently, there was some sort of breakdown in communication, and since they hadn't heard from us, they thought we were leaning toward The Learning Channel, one of the other networks who had expressed interest in us. We reassured them that we had not signed with anyone and were still interested in doing the show, and that's when they got real serious."

"Okay then," the person from HGTV responded. "Then we just have one final question: Do you guys have an agenda?"

The brothers made it clear that they did not have an agenda. They simply believed the Bible and what it says about marriage—wisdom that has been around for thousands of years going back to the Old Testament. They reiterated that they are not against gays, but believe that as Christians they have a right to accept what the Bible teaches about homosexuality, including that we are called to love all people regardless of their sexual orientation.

That seemed to do the trick. Up until that point, their offer from HGTV was a verbal offer. Within days of their conversation in Nashville, they received a written contract committing HGTV to the six initial episodes. Not only that, but HGTV made it clear they were eager to get started. They had done all their research and background checks on the brothers and now wanted to get going with the show, which would be called *Flip It Forward*.

Meanwhile, Jason and David continued to openly minister through their Bible studies and podcasts as well as speaking at events all over the country where they are open about their faith. They got a call from my team at Family Research Council, who asked them to speak at the conservative Values Voter Summit, and initially they wondered if speaking at such an event would upset the suits at HGTV.

"After thinking it over for about a minute we thought, *Forget that—we're speaking no matter what*," David recalled.

In April 2014, HGTV began filming the show, and after one of the first days of filming, an executive approached them and offered to take them out to dinner at one of the finest steak restaurants in Charlotte, North Carolina, and that's when it became clear what was truly at stake if Jesus was to be Lord of their lives.

The executive told them how he followed them on Facebook and Twitter and noticed they talk a lot about "Christian things," indicating that he was okay with that. But then he referred to one of David's tweets about his dad baptizing Norma Jean McCorvey, who was Jane Roe in the infamous *Roe v. Wade* Supreme Court case that legalized abortion, adding that he went too far by bringing this up.

They simply believed the Bible and what it says about marriage.

"It was at that moment right there sitting in Fleming's restaurant with a sizzling steak staring us in the face when we knew we had to answer a question: *Are you going to follow Jesus whatever the cost?* The fear inside of us wanted to say, *Hey—it's okay. We'll stop tweeting. Whatever it takes, we're going to keep the show because it will give us so much influence for Jesus.* But that was Satan luring us out of the fight, something we weren't about to let happen. Even as we further explained our beliefs to the executive, we knew it was over. No matter how much influence it would give us, we could not agree to let some television executive push us around." The executive basically told them they could be Christian; they just had to keep quiet about abortion. They politely made it clear that they couldn't do that.

After the meeting, the brothers compared notes. Both agreed that it was the Holy Spirit who filled them with enough courage to stand for Jesus. They also admitted to each other that they were crestfallen about losing the show. Not because they wanted to be superstars, but in David's words, "We wanted to use that huge platform to fight. We wanted to take down these strongholds of Satan and glorify God and see His kingdom advance. But we lost it. Lost the platform."

But for some reason, the executive called them later and told them they would move forward with the show, presenting it at an "upfront" in New York City, which was a way of attracting advertisers. And then he told them, "We just hope you don't get labeled as haters."

"We knew that eventually we would lose our platform, but since they were willing to continue, we thought we could at least use one or two episodes for the kingdom."

So they continued filming while HGTV presented the show to potential advertisers in New York, which led to yet another call from the HGTV executive. He reported that major advertisers loved the show, as did many of the other advertisers. But there was a problem. An organization known as Gay & Lesbian Alliance Against Defamation (GLAAD) expressed strong displeasure that HGTV was airing the show. But the executive felt they wouldn't be a serious problem. He would try to talk to them and explain that the Benham brothers were not haters, had sold houses to gays and lesbians, and in general were good people. But within twenty-four hours, a notice had been posted on the HGTV Facebook page that *Flip It Forward* was being reviewed, and the comments following the article literally blew up the page. Thousands of responses, all negative. Apparently GLAAD had mobilized their base, calling for an attack on HGTV—a massive online protest that David later described as a "well-orchestrated hit on traditional Christian values."

It was with a sick feeling in the pits of their stomachs that Jason and David showed up the next morning to shoot another episode. No one else on the set seemed to know what was happening behind the scenes, but once the shooting was over, their HGTV executive asked them to join him for a conference call with the brass of HGTV—the real movers and shakers of the network. They left the set, drove to Jason's home, and went into his bedroom to make the call.

"We knew this was serious, so we got down on our knees and prayed, pledging to God that we would never back down, never let anyone silence us or force us to turn away from our Christian values, regardless of the cost. Then we got on the conference call with New York, and the message was brief and to the point."

We just hope you don't get labeled as haters.

"Guys, we've decided to cancel the show."

And then another voice, someone from the executive team: "I'm speechless. I just can't believe this is happening."

The Benham brothers knew that HGTV had been bullied into their decision by GLAAD, so their fight wasn't with the network. In fact, after learning that their show had been canceled, here's how the brothers responded: "Thanks. We love you guys. We have nothing against you. Thank you for this opportunity. We trust God with our future. We know God's in control."

Over the next two weeks, the Benham brothers became one of the biggest stories in the news and on the Internet as they faced a firestorm of criticism—something like fifty-one million tweets about their story and the number one story on Facebook. Yet not more than a few prominent pastors went public to support the duo. Why? Because of fear. Fear of man. We all like to talk about how our country has abandoned its religious roots, but here was a chance to take a stand for two guys who refused to bow down to forces who hate Christian values, yet Christian leaders gave in to their fears.

"A lot of our friends went to their pastors asking them to support us, but they were told Christians need to be winsome," David lamented. "We so wanted to have those spiritual giants in our corner, but they never showed up."

The Enemy continues to attack them, as many of their clients have mysteriously pulled some of their business, but Jason and David have no regrets.

"We all have a choice. We can serve God or we can serve man. We chose God, and if we had it to do all over again, we'd make the same choice."

We chose God, and if we had it to do all over again, we'd make the same choice.

■ ■ ■

Is there not a cause? (1 Samuel 17:29)

David had a future. Samuel the prophet had come to his small, sleepy town of Bethlehem and, at the direction of the Lord, anointed David as the future king of Israel.

While he may not have understood all that Samuel had said to him and his father that day as the prophet poured the anointing oil on his head, David was not the same little shepherd boy. As Samuel anointed David, the Spirit of the Lord came upon him (1 Samuel 16:13). So I would venture to say that as he continued in his duties tending the sheep and occasionally serving in the court of the lame-duck king, Saul (verses 18–23), he was thinking of the future.

A devout worshiper of Jehovah, David was most probably thinking about how he could use this platform as king to impact the nation for the Lord. As king, people would listen to him. It wouldn't just be the sheep hearing his songs of praise; he would be able to lead all of Israel in worshiping God. That was the context of David's encounter with Goliath.

David had already been anointed king when he was transporting the MREs (Meals Ready to Eat) of his day—cheese and bread—to the battlefield for his brothers, who were a part of the army of Israel that was in a standoff with the Philistines. For forty days the champion of the Philistines, a nine-foot, nine-inch giant named Goliath, had taunted the Israelites by mocking God and challenging one of them to a duel. They had all politely declined, including Saul, because "they were dismayed and greatly afraid" (1 Samuel 17:11).

It's a good thing David didn't have political advisors at that point, because they would have told him to play it safe. I can just imagine their words to him: "David, you will have a platform soon enough; there is too much at stake to get involved in this giant business. Why not let one of these professionals take on the giant and you stay focused on your future?"

Think about it. Why should he risk his future as king? After all, this was Saul's problem. In fact, if Saul was disgraced by the Philistine army, this situation could expedite David's ascendancy to the throne. Why bail him out?

Everything might be jeopardized by getting involved. Just think of all the good things David would be able to do in the future as king that would now be put at risk by taking on this giant. This was foolishness, because David didn't have a snowball's chance in taking out this battle-hardened behemoth.

David has not been the only one to be faced with such a choice. The Benham brothers were the next reality-TV superstars.

It wasn't the money and the fame that appealed to them, but the opportunities that such a platform would provide for them to do good. All they had to do was play it safe. Let someone else fight the spiritual and cultural giants of our day, and the path would be clear for them to share God's love on the national stage.

David didn't have a snowball's chance in taking out this battle-hardened behemoth.

Here is what it came down to for David, for the Benham brothers, and for every follower of Jesus who is tempted to play it safe: "And David said . . . 'Is there not a cause?'" (verse 29). It was a rhetorical question to which the answer was obvious.

Yes, there was a cause. It was a cause greater than David's future. It was a cause that transcended David's own comfort and convenience. It was a cause worth dying for. The cause was God.

God's own reputation, the essence of who He was, was being challenged by a giant in defying the armies of the living God. This is the same type of righteous indignation that led Jesus to turn over the tables on the money changers in the temple (John 2:13–17). When you have a cause that is greater than yourself, you will step out in faith.

Is there not a cause in our day as cultural and political giants continue to defy God and mock His people?

MAKING IT REAL

1. Are you playing not to lose rather than playing to win? Are you avoiding the risks that are inherited when living for Jesus? Proverbs 26:13 says, "The lazy man says, 'There is a lion in the road! A fierce lion is in the streets!'" Is the lazy person who goes nowhere in life the one who avoids risks? Do you want to really serve the Lord? Don't run from the giants or hide from the lions!

2. Be honest with yourself. Are there any giants in your life that you are avoiding? Like Saul and his army, have you allowed fear of a giant to paralyze you?

3. Exercise your faith. As David and the Benhams did, take a moment and recount what God has done in your life (1 Samuel 17:37). List two or three occasions in your life where God gave you the victory.

4. Like David, you have to choose to let your faith triumph over your fears. Make David's prayer in Psalm 23 your prayer.

Yea, though I walk through the valley
      of the shadow of death,
I will fear no evil;
For You are with me;
Your rod and Your staff, they comfort me.

You prepare a table before me in the presence
      of my enemies;
You anoint my head with oil;
My cup runs over.
Surely goodness and mercy shall follow me
All the days of my life;
And I will dwell in the house of the LORD
Forever. (verses 4–6)

9

The Right Way to Fight

If you've ever attended a high-school football game, you've seen it. At the far end of the field, the home team gathers in a circle, amped up on an exhilarating mix of fear and courage. Somewhere inside that mass of shoulder pads and helmets, the team captain cranks up the adrenaline, imploring his troops with a dozen different clichéd ways of saying "We can do it!" A week of grueling practices and team meetings wedged between classes and homework are temporarily forgotten. The battle beckons, punctuated by stadium lights, the heart-pumping staccato of the band's drum line, and the coach's locker-room charge. These young warriors are ready! A crescendo of expectation builds as the cheerleaders unroll a giant banner painted in the school colors, the signal for the pep squad to rush out onto the field to form a human tunnel of support. In seconds, the captain will slash through that banner, leading his battalion into what, in Texas, is almost a sacred ritual: Friday Night Lights.

Except on *this* Friday night someone in the crowd was taking note of that banner held taut for the players to break through and sprint past their screaming fans. Instead of the usual "Go Lions!

Smash the Bulldogs!" a different message welcomed player and fan alike to the much-awaited Friday-night contest: "I can do all things through Christ, which strengthens!" That someone taking notes scribbled the words onto a piece of paper as evidence— proof that the school had crossed the infamous line of "separation between state and church." After the game, the silent observer contacted the Freedom From Religion Foundation, more than a thousand miles away in Madison, Wisconsin. The battle on the football field would pale compared to what was in store for the salt-of-the-earth folks of Kountze, Texas, including one blond, athletic cheerleader: Rebekah Richardson.

The Freedom From Religion Foundation does its best to live up to its name. Or maybe *down* to it. They're the ones who threaten to sue cities if they don't remove "dangerous" Nativity scenes from public property or ban the very practice that Congress has engaged in from its beginning—opening meetings with prayer. They have even gone to the point of threatening to turn pastors into the IRS if they urge parishioners to vote. They have even tried to stop restaurants from offering a 10 percent discount to anyone bringing in a church bulletin. As if saving a dollar on the bacon-and-eggs special at Prudhomme's Lost Cajun Kitchen in Pennsylvania or saving a few dollars on a pizza at Bailey's Pizza in Searcy, Arkansas, puts our nation at risk of becoming a theocracy.

So no doubt when someone from Kountze, Texas, contacted them about the banners, the organization licked their collective chops and went after Superintendent Kevin Weldon. Instead of telling them to mind their business in Wisconsin, he consulted with his school district's lawyers. Nothing like this had ever happened in the quiet community of Kountze, and he wanted to get it right. The lawyers determined that this student-initiated attempt to replace a battle cry with ancient wisdom was too dangerous to allow. He sent out his decree to the schools in his district.

From now on, stick to "Pulverize the Pirates!" or something less offensive than Bible verses! "We were in the locker room one afternoon after school when the principal came on the PA system and announced that no one could display banners with Bible verses on

> **I knew that darkness and light can't coexist in the world, but it really seemed unfair.**

them," recalled Rebekah. "At the time, I wasn't that upset. I knew that darkness and light can't coexist in the world, but it really seemed unfair because all of us had been taught in school that the Constitution protects our beliefs."

Rebekah, who was seventeen at the time, had spent her entire life in the comfortable surroundings of Kountze. As had her dad, who owned a heavy-equipment business, and her grandfather. Most of her friends had done the same, growing up in the small town northeast of Houston. This was the kind of community where everyone knew each other, watched out for each other, and did their best to live honest, law-abiding lives. And like just about everyone in Kountze, Rebekah had grown up in church.

"All my friends and I started going to church practically from the day we were born," she laughed. "I think we all were in church nurseries the first Sunday after we were born. But as we grew up, church became extremely important to us. We didn't all go to the same church, but all of us believed in God and were taught from the Bible."

Rebekah made a profession of faith at an early age, but as she matured she began to see that growing up in a town where everyone goes to church has its disadvantages. Going to church becomes more of a good habit or "the right thing to do" than a desire to worship and obey Christ. All of us who were taken to church at an early age reach a point where we have to determine if our faith is truly our own, rather than something we do because it's expected of us. Rebekah described it as an "empty religion." Others call it "cultural Christianity," meaning we put on the appearance of faith just to blend in. So in Kountze, Texas, the way to blend in is to go to church. In fact, a lot of American Christians just blend in and lack real conviction, which is exactly why the Freedom From Religion Foundation is often so confident they can intimidate Christians into silence. The radical secularist group thought that silencing a bunch of high-school cheerleaders would be an easy task. But they grossly underestimated Rebekah and her squad.

"During my freshman year, I began to see that being a Christian was more than just going to church. I also began to realize what Christ had done for me when He gave His life for me on the cross. I understood that because of His example, I have a responsibility to treat others the way Jesus treated others—both those I agree with and those I disagree with."

In fact, it was that change in attitude that initially led Rebekah and her friends to alter the message of their banners.

"This wasn't something we deliberated about or did to cause problems for anyone. We just thought it would be better to put an encouraging message out there instead of slandering the other team. We were all Christians anyway, so we had no idea that it would offend anyone."

For about two weeks, she was right. No one complained. In fact, everyone seemed to appreciate the cheerleaders' efforts to encourage and uplift players and fans alike from both teams. But as Rebekah would soon learn, all it takes is one person to silence the beliefs of others. It's important to note that the decision to put Bible verses on the banners came solely from the cheerleaders. While they had an advisor who was an employee of the school, that person had nothing to do with the decision. The girls came up with the idea while at cheerleading camp over the summer.

> I began to see that being a Christian was more than just going to church.

I've never been to a cheerleading camp, but I imagine it went something like this. After a three-hour practice in a stuffy gymnasium, the cheerleaders took a break outside, sitting in the shade of a tree as the east Texas wind offered welcome relief.

"Hey, we need to get a banner ready for our first game. Any ideas?"

"Can't we just use some of the same ones we used last year?"

"Naw, that's so lame."

"Yeah, but how many ways can we say 'Smear the other team'?"

"Maybe we could say something more positive—something that would be more of an encouragement."

"Like what?"

"Well, look at all those Bible verses we had to memorize in Sunday school. Some of those are pretty cool. And inspiring too."

Okay, maybe it didn't happen exactly that way, but Rebekah assured me that no one from her school's staff had anything to do with the banners. The messages were strictly student initiated. This was a group of high-school students who chose inspiring messages from the ancient wisdom of the Bible, grabbed some paint brushes and tempera paint, and scrawled the messages on paper that they would stretch across the end zone for everyone to see. They even used their own paint and paper. In other words, this wasn't an employee or official from a publicly funded school trying to force anyone to accept a particular faith or worldview. Just a handful of teenagers who decided inspiring others would be better than name calling and insulting the opposing team.

Rebekah and her friends were about to learn that when you publicly stand up for truth, though, there's oftentimes a cost.

After the superintendent told them they couldn't display Bible verses on their banners, the cheerleaders and their parents had to figure out what to do. One option was to go with the flow and follow the school district's directive. But none of the cheerleaders thought that was right. Didn't the Constitution protect their right of free speech and to exercise their belief in God? The other option was to fight the decision, but what would that mean? They were just kids. How does a student challenge the superintendent without getting into a lot of trouble?

After meeting with their parents, they decided to seek an injunction from Hardin County district court judge Steve Thomas, requesting permission to continue encouraging football fans with uplifting messages. They were represented by attorneys from the Liberty Institute in nearby Plano, Texas, who argued that the school was violating the students' constitutional right to free speech. Attorneys for the district claimed the signs were illegal, because they amounted to an endorsement of religion by the government, since the school is funded by taxpayers.

But before the case could be argued in court, the cheerleaders had a big decision to make. A game was coming up, and the superintendent and principal made it clear they couldn't put Bible verses on their banners. The judge had given them an injunction, meaning they could go ahead with the posters until the case could be tried on the merits. But how would the community respond? What would other students say? And more important to Rebekah, what would be the best way to honor God?

How does a student challenge the superintendent without getting into a lot of trouble?

"The media attention was unbelievable as camera crews showed up at school to interview us. We knew they would be at the game, and all that attention made us nervous. We always prayed together before games, and that week we prayed almost every day. Our prayer was not that we would win our case in court, but that through everything we did, God would be glorified. We ultimately decided to go ahead with the Bible verses on the banner, but my real hope was that people would look at what we were doing and see Christ and not people who just want their own way."

The game went on without incident, as once again no one for a hundred miles seemed to object to seeing a Bible verse at a football game. In fact, a lot of people knew that the superintendent had tried to squelch the Bible banners and made it a point to express their appreciation to the cheerleaders. But now the case was in a judge's hands, and not the residents of Kountze. In the back of Rebekah's mind a daunting question loomed: *What should I do if the judge rules against us?*

"I talked it over with my parents, and they told me they would support me whatever I decided to do," Rebekah told me. "I think they wanted it to be my decision and not something I would choose because of their influence."

As the much-anticipated court date approached, the town demonstrated their support for the cheerleaders. Churches sponsored rallies and prayer services to stand in solidarity with them. Someone launched a Facebook page that quickly registered more than forty-five thousand followers, pretty significant given the fact that the population of Kountze, Texas, was only 2,123.

Not everyone in government thought the girls had violated the law or advised that the atheists' demands should be met. Greg Abbott, then the Texas attorney general, not only spoke out publicly on the girls' behalf, he wrote a letter of support to the judge.

The battle lines were drawn as Rebekah and her cheerleaders boldly entered the courtroom with their attorneys, Hiram Sasser and David Starnes. Outside the courthouse, it seemed one sided as more than eighty fans—parents and other supporters—showed up with their own posters in support. One quoted Scripture and referenced the Kountze High School mascot: "The wicked flee though no one pursues, but the righteous are as bold as a lion!"

> The battle lines were drawn as Rebekah and her cheerleaders boldly entered the courtroom.

Inside, the district's lawyers tried to build a case that the cheerleaders represented the school and thus could not express their personal religious beliefs. They cited a previous decision that banned student-initiated prayers over a loudspeaker during football games, ruling them unconstitutional. Liberty Institute lawyers fired back, citing a 1969 ruling that allowed students to wear armbands protesting the Vietnam War. They also reminded the judge that because the cheerleaders made the posters on their own time using their own materials, the district had no right to tell them what to put on the banners.

The judge's decision was swift and clear, but short lived. He ruled that the banners were constitutional, but the school district immediately appealed the decision, essentially putting the entire case on hold. And this time, the opposition to the banners widened. The American Civil Liberties Union; the Anti-Defamation League; the Interfaith Alliance Foundation; Muslim Advocates; the Union for Reform Judaism; Hadassah, the Women's Zionist Organization of America; the Hindu American Foundation; Americans United for Separation of Church and State; and the Sikh Coalition all joined to oppose the cheerleaders.

"We decided to just go ahead and put Bible verses on our banners," Rebekah explained. "Everyone was confused about what was going on, and the media attention was pretty intense all through the rest of the football season. Our decision in favor of the Bible took its toll as we spent so much time giving depositions, meeting with the lawyers to understand what was happening, and being interviewed by the media."

> Our motives and manner are just as important as, if not more important than, our actions.

What stands out for me about Rebekah, however, is how she wanted all the attention and strife to be used by God for His glory. Our motives and manner are just as important as, if not more important than, our actions. Why are we taking the stand we are taking? Is it so that we will be seen, or that Christ will be seen? Are we honoring the Lord by how we are treating those who oppose us? Sometimes, people get caught up in the fury of these conflicts and respond in such a way that their manner does not reflect the love we are told to have for those who oppose us (Matthew 5:44). Rebekah, who also ran cross-country and played on the varsity tennis team, demonstrated a spiritual maturity that I don't even see consistently in older Christians who stand up for what they believe.

"I didn't have a problem with the people who opposed us," she explained. "They don't know Christ, so they can't possibly understand why the Bible is so important to me. Even when they said things that were unkind or untrue, it didn't really bother me because without the Holy Spirit, they were incapable of love, truth, and compassion. It wasn't hard for me to extend grace to them."

Rebekah's bigger challenge was extending grace to those who professed Christ but treated the opposition uncharitably.

"It was harder for me to show grace to people on our side who treated the opposition maliciously. God had to teach me to be just as graceful to those who are still learning and aren't representing Christ very well."

Wise words from such a young ambassador for Christ. As it turned out, her greatest "fear" in taking a stand was not the rejection or ridicule she might face, or even the threat of arrest from breaking a law. Her greatest fear was to fail to represent her Lord during a time of intense trial and tribulation.

"I was really out there, and knew that a lot of people all across the nation—maybe even the world—would be watching. I wanted so badly for Christ to be represented well. I didn't want to take a stand for my faith and then have others be able to say that my life and behavior didn't match up to that faith."

Rebekah gets it. If the stand we take is motivated by a need to "win" an argument or prevail over those we oppose, we may win the battle but lose in the long run. But if our convictions are based on our love for Jesus and obedience to His Word, our actions, though unpopular, can actually point unbelievers to the Savior. And when you think of it, the best way to eliminate the things happening in society that must sadden Jesus is to draw more people into His kingdom. Show them a better way in hopes that they might want what we have: the love and forgiveness of Christ.

Rebekah summarized her view this way: "There's a way to take a stand for your faith without attacking others. That doesn't mean that we back down from our convictions, but that we hold to them in a loving way—in a way that respects even those who oppose us." As it turns out, every follower of Christ is admonished to take this very approach. The apostle Paul gave very similar advice to Timothy: "And the Lord's servant must not quarrel; instead, he must be kind to everyone, able to teach, not resentful" (2 Timothy 2:24, NIV). For Rebekah Richardson and her Christian classmates, this isn't just a quaint saying; it is their worldview.

> There's a way to take a stand for your faith without attacking others.

As of this writing, the case is still in limbo. Rebekah graduated and is now studying at the University of Houston, majoring in nursing and liberal-arts studies. She and her fellow cheerleaders never backed down—displaying God's Word on their hand-painted banners every Friday night for the rest of the football season.

And for the first time in forty years, the team made it to the playoffs.

The righteous truly are bold as a lion!

...

> Nebuchadnezzar spoke, saying, "Blessed be the God of
> Shadrach, Meshach, and Abed-Nego, who sent His Angel
> and delivered His servants who trusted in Him, and they
> have frustrated the king's word, and yielded their bodies,
> that they should not serve nor worship any god except
> their own God!" (Daniel 3:28)

Years ago—in fact, over twenty-five hundred years ago—there was another cheering squad that actually received a lot of heat for not cheering. You may have heard of the story of the three Hebrew young men Shadrach, Meshach, and Abed-Nego. These three along with Daniel, of the lions' den notoriety, had been carried away captive from their homes in Jerusalem when they were children to the capital of the Chaldean empire, Babylon. In Babylon they were taught the language, educated, trained, and prepared to be leaders of the vast empire under the control of Nebuchadnezzar.

Like Rebekah and her companions, the three Hebrew young men faced a test. It wasn't a multiple-choice exam; it was a test of conviction, a test of whether or not when the heat was on, they would melt or stand with their trust totally in God.

Sometime after assuming their leadership assignments, Shadrach, Meshach, and Abed-Nego were summoned back to Babylon for a pep rally to unveil a huge idol created by Nebuchadnezzar. Word was sent out that when the band struck up the king's anthem, everyone, from everywhere, was commanded to fall down and worship the golden idol. The consequences of failing to fall were made quite clear. Those who did not fall down and worship the idol would be immediately cast "into the midst of a burning fiery furnace" (Daniel 3:6).

Before you dismiss as laughable in the twenty-first century the notion that someone would be forced to bow down to a gold-plated idol that probably resembled a prop from a 1950s B-movie, think about it. Do we not have objects or ideas that are treated in ways similar to the idols and gods of ancient days? One could make a plausible argument that secularism, the exclusion of religion from public life, has by our government's allegiance become like a deity that we are forced to bow to in the public space.

You may think that such a statement is an exaggeration of our present situation as compared to the days of Nebuchadnezzar, but was that not in effect what Rebekah, the other cheerleaders, the football team, and even the community had forced upon them? They were told to make their orthodox Christian views, shared by the vast majority of the community, subservient to the demands of a radical secularist organization located more than one thousand miles away. What happened to the freedom of speech? Where did the rights of conscience and free exercise of religion go?

> Do we not have objects or ideas that are treated in ways similar to the idols and gods of ancient days?

Unfortunately, many today are dismissing this existential threat to our core freedoms as nothing more than a groundless conspiracy theory. The evidence is more than conclusive. Visit www.frc.org/clearpresentdanger for the attacks on religious freedom in our nation's military and www.frc.org/hostilityreport to read about the growing hostility toward the Christian faith in America. If you are not just a believer in Jesus Christ, but a follower, I encourage you to prepare yourself by considering how Shadrach, Meshach, and Abed-Nego responded to their test. *Your* test may come sooner than you think.

The Freedom From Religion Foundation doesn't date back to the time of Nebuchadnezzar, but their predecessors were there and they were all too eager to carry word to the king that there were some individuals violating the decree to bow down to the state's idol.

The trio was summarily hauled before the king, the charges stated, and Nebuchadnezzar asked, "Is it true, Shadrach, Meshach, and Abed-Nego, that you do not serve my gods or worship the gold image which I have set up?" (Daniel 3:14). He then proceeded to give them a second chance: "Now if you are ready at the time you hear the sound of the horn, flute, harp, lyre, and psaltery, in symphony with all kinds of music, and you fall down and worship the image which I have made, good! But if you do not worship, you shall be cast immediately into the midst of a burning fiery furnace. And who is the god who will deliver you from my hands?" (verse 15).

Notice that the king extended them a second chance. Was Nebuchadnezzar going soft? I doubt it. Actually we don't know for certain, but I would venture to say it was because the king either knew these three personally or by reputation as men of professional excellence and uncompromising conduct. Being that such men were in short supply, he didn't want to literally fire them if he didn't have to!

Think for just a moment what had to be going through their minds as their faces grew flush from the radiating heat of the nearby scorching furnace. Do you think they began to entertain the idea of backing down and just bowing to the idol, rationalizing the decision as just bowing on the outside, but on the inside they would remain committed to the one true God? After all, just think of all the good they could do in their positions of influence. All of that would be lost if they refused to bow. Maybe they thought, *Do you really think God wanted us to go through all those years of training and preparation only to die because we would not bow down for a few minutes to a gaudy-looking gold idol?*

The biblical account would suggest that they had already counted the cost and made up their minds: they would not bow. "We have no need to answer you in this matter" (verse 16). They had already prepared for this day of testing, deciding to place their trust in the one true God. "Our God whom we serve is able to deliver us from the burning fiery furnace, and He will deliver us from your hand, O king" (verse 17). Whether by miracle or martyrdom, they were confident that they would triumph because they had placed their trust in the Lord.

We must, as hundreds of thousands of followers of Jesus before us have, be willing to pay the price when we stand for Jesus in the face of anti-Christian leaders (Matthew 12:30). The price varies. For some it is little more than the inconvenience of having to stand up and defend your right to express your belief in God. For others the price of standing up for Jesus may be a tarnished reputation. It could come in the form of lost friends, or even the termination from a coveted job or position. There are even those in our day, like the men, women, and even children in Iraq and Syria, who by refusing to deny Jesus, are being martyred by radical Islamists.

> There are even those in our day who by refusing to deny Jesus are being martyred by radical Islamists.

In Shadrach, Meshach, and Abed-Nego's case, God chose to display His divinity not in the power of martyrdom, but through the power of a miracle. Not only did God deliver the three from the furnace, He walked with them through the fire.

Their triumph over evil was indisputable. Nebuchadnezzar had witnessed God honoring the trust the three young Hebrews had placed in Him by literally walking with them in the fire. The impact upon the king was profound as he not only reversed his command to worship his dead idol; he decreed that no one could speak anything amiss about the living God! How did it turn out for the three recusants who were willing to give their all in standing for the Lord, including their very lives? Not only were the three pardoned, they were promoted!

MAKING IT REAL

1. Do you just believe in Jesus or do you follow Jesus? There is a big difference. The apostle James wrote, "You believe that there is one God. You do well. Even the demons believe— and tremble!" (James 2:19). Jesus has called us not to just believe in Him, but to follow Him.

2. Rebekah Richardson, like the Hebrew trio, knew this was not about her and the cheerleading squad. It was about the God they served. We need to make sure our stand for Jesus honors Jesus! You might remember the old adage that two wrongs don't make a right. Make sure your motives are

right, and make sure you communicate your conviction in a way that respects those whom God has placed in authority, even though they may be ungodly and dead wrong in their demands (Romans 13:1).

3. The cost of discipleship, of following Jesus, is going up. Increasingly, living openly as a Christian, refusing to bow to the "idols" and "gods" of our age, you will find yourself in conflict with some of the rulers of this age. If you wait until the conflict is upon you to decide how you will respond, it's too late. Like Shadrach, Meshach, and Abed-Nego, you need to make your choice now (Joshua 24:15). To whom are you going to bow? The "gods" of this age or the God of the ages? Pray and ask God to give you the courage and wisdom to make the right choice.

10

If You Pray, You Go to Jail

Have you ever wondered what you would do if it was against the law to practice your Christian faith? For example, during the French Revolution, public and private worship was outlawed; hundreds of priests who refused to stop serving communion were executed. Even now in Saudi Arabia, it is illegal to publicly worship any deity but Allah, and any Muslim who converts to Christianity may legally be punished by death. Even as I write this in 2015, we are aware on almost a daily basis of followers of Christ being tortured and beheaded by ISIS in the Middle East.

More recently—and closer to home—if you were a high-school student and offered a prayer at the end of your graduation speech, you could go to jail!

What would you do, knowing that obeying your conscience could send you to a cell with violent criminals ready to welcome you? And that a criminal record could keep you out of the college you wanted to attend or prevent you from getting a good job?

Great theoretical questions, right? And if you're like me, you would probably say, "Of course I'd choose to follow God no matter what the cost."

For Angela Hildenbrand, though, this isn't a make-believe "What if?" This is the real deal, in the United States of America where hostility toward the Christian faith is increasing. Even in her rural Texas town of Castroville, where everyone knew each other and on any given Sunday most town folk were in church.

Angela was born to Timothy and Sandra Hildenbrand, the third child of four kids in a home richly influenced by their Catholic Christian faith. Timothy, a petroleum engineer, leads a gas-exploration company, and prior to starting their family, Sandra also worked in the petroleum industry as a land-management expert. Both parents taught their children to integrate their faith into everything they did, whether it was at home, with friends, in the classroom, or on the athletic field. Angela, who is currently studying theology at Ave Maria University, credits her parents for influencing her early faith development.

"My parents expected me to be a good steward of the gifts God had given me, and they also sent us to Catholic elementary school, where we received a sound formation and where faith was the center of our education," Angela explained. "Both in our home and at school I received a great foundation for my faith that prepared me for the challenges I would face in middle school and high school when I went to public school."

But at some point, those of us who are raised in Christian homes need to choose for ourselves whether or not to accept the faith that we've been taught, and for Angela that happened through the influence of a Christian summer sports camp. It was there that she grew into her own faith, impressed with the counselors who gave up higher-paying summer jobs just to invest in the spiritual lives of the campers.

"My summers at camp really shaped me as a Christian," Angela told me. "Even during the school year I could call my counselors when I had questions. They encouraged me in my walk with Jesus, and that kind of support and accountability are really vital to our faith."

As a young Christian, Angela was all in. She volunteered to lead spiritual retreats for kids in the community. She became active in the Fellowship of Christian Athletes (FCA). And she started a Bible study at her school—Medina Valley High School.

At some point, those of us who are raised in Christian homes need to choose for ourselves whether or not to accept the faith that we've been taught.

"I had been helped so much by my counselors at camp that I was inspired to help others grow in their faith."

Even a setback in her sophomore year did not discourage this vibrant young student-athlete from following Jesus.

"At our first track meet of the season—my first triple jump approach—I felt a stabbing pain in my hip, and for the rest of the season, I was running through tears. It kept getting worse, and despite imaging scans and X-rays, the doctors didn't know what was wrong. I tried to keep resting, rehabilitating it, and competing, but despite my best efforts, my season ended with my collapsing after crossing the finish line of the two-hundred-meter dash at the district meet. I didn't know it at the time, but halfway through that first race I had torn the cartilage inside of my hip socket."

The injury plagued her throughout the season, and by the time basketball season rolled around the following year, it wasn't any better. Still, she tried her best to play through the pain. This lanky sophomore, tough as the plains of southwest Texas, wasn't about to let an injury keep her on the bench. She gave her all to the Lady Panthers, taking little time off before the track season rolled around. But when she finally got outdoors on the track, each race ended in excruciating pain and bitter disappointment—the pain and growing cartilage tear (still undiagnosed) sapped the power and speed she'd once had, and after the last meet, Angela reluctantly made one of the toughest decisions of her young life: her athletic career was over.

"This was a very difficult time for me, because I absolutely love sports. But I could see that God was working on me through all the pain and disappointment. He showed me that I had placed too much emphasis on my identity as an athlete. I volunteered to help my coaches during my senior year, and that helped me cope with not being able to compete. But I also was able to get more involved in music, and started taking a bigger role in FCA as a worship leader, sharing my witness to other athletes in our meetings. Having to give up sports was painful, but it expedited my spiritual journey and led me to see that God was calling me to music ministry."

When God closes doors for us, it's easy to get discouraged. Angela's spiritually mature response to this setback reminded me of Isaiah Austin, the Baylor University basketball star, who just four days before the NBA draft was told he would never play basketball again due to a previously unknown medical condition. Deprived of what would have been a lucrative professional career, Austin tweeted his followers: "Toughest days of my life. But not the last! Life goes on. GOD IS STILL GREAT!" This kind of bravery is rare in young people today, but what was in store for Angela would require even more courage and tenacity than missing her senior basketball and track seasons.

Going into her final semester, Angela's grades placed her second in her class of about two hundred classmates. Apparently, Mom and Dad's emphasis on always doing your best paid off. With nine weeks to graduation, Angela learned that she had surged into the top spot in her class and would graduate as valedictorian. That remarkable honor brought with it yet another opportunity: she would deliver the valedictory address to her fellow students and all the parents and relatives who would pack Medina Valley's football stadium to send off the class of 2011.

When God closes doors for us, it's easy to get discouraged.

"That's when things got a little crazy," she recalled.

About two weeks before graduation, Angela and a few of her classmates who had been selected to speak were called to a meeting at the school. That in itself wasn't unusual, as school officials usually just wanted to make sure they were prepared.

"They basically told us that we were the leaders of our class and that they trusted us, and if we needed any help they would be there for us. They also mentioned that they would need to see copies of what we planned to say, which seemed reasonable and was standard."

But then, one week before graduation, they were called into another meeting and learned that a family who described themselves as agnostics had filed a lawsuit aimed at prohibiting any public prayers during the graduation ceremony. Medina Valley had a long tradition of beginning graduation with an invocation and ending it with a benediction—all delivered voluntarily by students.

"The administration told us not to be alarmed and that they would keep us posted on the lawsuit—one they intended to fight."

Angela left the meeting confident everything would turn out okay, but the next day, US District Court Judge Fred Biery handed down his ruling. Not only would student prayers be banned from the graduation ceremony, but any mention of Jesus, Lord, or even the word *prayer*. Curiously, the judge also ruled that the word *amen* was also off limits to the students. In what he probably thought was an act of generous inclusiveness, he ruled that it would be permissible for a student to wear a yarmulke or kneel toward Mecca.

Angela could hardly believe what she was hearing.

"It seemed so outrageous. Not just that the judge had ruled against prayer, but even more so because he favored other religions over Christianity. As a high schooler I could tell his argument was flawed, even from a secular point of view."

From what she could determine, the majority of students and faculty at her high school shared her disbelief and disappointment, though a few took the opportunity to praise the decision. School officials were cautious about what they said publicly because an appeal was in process, but Angela could tell they weren't happy.

As she left the meeting, Angela began thinking about what she should do. It didn't seem right or fair that her two friends who had been selected to pray—friends who attended her church—were deprived of the opportunity to give the invocation and benediction. They weren't employees of the school, but private citizens who believed in God and wanted to honor Him at this important event in their lives. Yet school officials had no choice but to reluctantly scratch them from the program. Initially, as she prepared her speech, Angela had not intended to close it with a prayer, but once it became clear that the invocation and benediction had been canceled, she began to consider doing something that could get her into serious trouble.

"I had seen a copy of the ruling, and it was clear that anyone who violated it would be incarcerated. To be honest, the thought of going to jail scared me—to be sent to San Antonio and thrown into a cell with gang members and other criminals, some who had committed violent crimes. An eighteen-year-old girl in that environment would be an easy target. I also knew that having a criminal record could hurt my chances of getting into college or getting a job."

> She began to consider doing something that could get her into serious trouble.

After the meeting, Angela met her dad in the parking lot of the high school. Like any good dad, he could see the disappointment in his daughter's body language and gave her a big hug. After a few moments, she told her dad that she thought she might end her speech with a prayer, defying the court order and inviting whatever punishment that would bring. Assuming the role of counselor, he did his best not to push her one way or the other. He understood that this was a pivotal moment in her young life and that as a young adult, she had to stand upon her own convictions. Just as she—and every one of us—had to decide on her own if she wanted to follow Christ, she now had to decide if she was willing to pay the price for following Him.

"I prayed a lot about what I should do, and God seemed to

lead me to think about St. Paul and what it was like for him and the other early church leaders who faced persecution and even death because of their faith in Christ. The more I prayed and meditated on Scripture, I knew that the same Spirit of God who was with them would be with me. If God was calling me to pray at my graduation, He would be faithful to provide me with the courage to obey Him. I overcame my fear by placing my trust in the Lord and abandoning myself to His goodness and providence."

Meanwhile, the judge's ruling ignited a firestorm of media attention that put tiny Castroville in the crosshairs of those who would love to see Christianity removed from our schools. With the prayers off the program, the next likely target was Angela.

> I overcame my fear by placing my trust in the Lord.

Because she had always been open about her faith and had filed an emergency motion for intervention to join the lawsuit as a third party, opponents to religious freedom suspected she might try to sneak something into her speech and were desperate to make sure that didn't happen. To no one's surprise, they took the cowardly approach. School officials received a chilling message: "If Angela Hildenbrand prays at graduation, she better watch out." For her safety, police provided a round-the-clock escort. It was also around this time that representatives from the Liberty Institute, an organization devoted solely to protecting religious liberty in America, agreed to help Angela with her appeal against the judge's ruling.

"During the week leading up to graduation, I hardly left the house except to do media interviews, and when I did, the police were always close by."

Rumors swirled that opponents to a student-led prayer planned to attend the ceremony, adding to the already anticipated huge crowd. Security was doubled, and Angela was asked not to attend the rehearsal on the night before the Saturday event. That's when it all came crashing down on her.

"With all that was going on, I still hadn't practiced my speech, and not being able to go to the rehearsal just added to my anxiety. Not only that, but I was also scheduled to sing the national anthem at graduation, but because I'd hardly slept for days and had to do so many interviews, my voice was hoarse and I wasn't sure I'd even be able to get through it. My grandpa had passed away just weeks earlier, and it made me so sad to know that he wouldn't be there to see me graduate. And then there was the possibility of going to jail. It was just too much. I started crying and praying to God for strength and peace—that I would have the courage to do what I needed to do and the humility to do it out of love so that everyone would see I wasn't trying to draw attention to myself or to spite anyone."

As she had done many times before, Angela turned to Scripture to bolster her courage. Two verses became especially encouraging, her constant companions throughout the confusion and fear of trying to do the right thing:

- "Be strong and of good courage, do not fear nor be afraid of them; for the LORD your God, He is the One who goes with you. He will not leave you nor forsake you" (Deuteronomy 31:6).
- "In this world you will have trouble. But take heart! I have overcome the world" (John 16:33, NIV).

"I consider myself a well-behaved child," she laughed. "I've always wanted to do the right thing—I've never even been to detention. And here I was about to intentionally violate a court order. Yeah, it shook me up, but more important than that law was God's law, so even if it might mean breaking the law, my primary loyalty is to the kingdom of heaven."

There's another verse Angela might have considered: "Commit to the LORD whatever you do, and he will establish your plans" (Proverbs 16:3, NIV). I believe God honors our obedience. Always. Maybe not always in the way we think He should, but choosing to obey God over man always puts us right in the center of God's will—no better place to be.

After her meltdown, Angela was about to turn in for the night when the phone rang. Knowing that it could be yet another anonymous threat, her dad answered it, and from the look on his face, Angela could see that it was anything but a threat.

"Our appeal was granted," he beamed.

The Fifth Circuit Court of Appeals had overturned Judge Biery's ruling. Angela would be able to pray and not go to jail. She was ecstatic.

"I was so excited, not just for myself, but the circuit court's ruling set a precedent for all other public schools in Texas and a few neighboring states as well. It was so amazing to see how God took Judge Biery's efforts to cut down the faithful and turned it around to help even more people than any initial efforts could have."

She might have been in the clear legally, but the new ruling only fanned the flames for that vocal minority opposed to religious freedom for our students. She woke up Saturday morning to increased concerns for her safety. She learned from her friends that they would be allowed to give the invocation and benediction, but that didn't change Angela's plans. She hadn't told anyone but her parents of her plans to pray at the end of her speech because she didn't want to implicate her friends as "accomplices."

But later as she headed out the door on her way to her graduation, she knew what she would do.

"I was still afraid because I knew I could be a target for an out-of-town radical, but I was excited to be an ambassador for Christ. Besides, along with my police escort, my brother would be running the sound system about twenty feet away from the podium. He's a football player and I knew he would have my back."

I was still afraid, but I was excited to be an ambassador for Christ.

She smiled to herself as one of her friends gave the invocation, and then belted out her rendition of the national anthem. She hardly heard the words of the school superintendent and other school officials as they spoke to the crowd because she was silently praying to collect herself. Soon she was introduced, and it was Angela's time to take her stand. She walked confidently to the podium, delivered her speech without a hitch, and then closed with a brief prayer.

"Amen!" shouted about five thousand people in unison.

"It was such a cool moment. Everyone stood and clapped for the longest time, and while I recognized they were commending me for what I had done, more than that I think everybody came together at that moment to stand for Christ in a world where that's becoming countercultural."

Despite her strong faith, Angela confided to me that she had always wondered what she would do if her faith was really on the line. Would she obey God or yield to man's ways? With all the threats and the potential consequences of violating a court order, no one would have blamed her for leaving a prayer out of her speech and moving on with her life. Fear can do that to you. But faith always trumps fear.

"You wonder sometimes, *When it comes down to the wire, will I be strong? When the consequences of obeying Him are scary, will I still obey?* This whole experience affirmed for me that I have been given the gift of faith and that God will always give me the grace and strength to say yes to Him."

Her yes preserved the rights of other students to live out their faith too. At least for now. There will be other challenges—other efforts to silence Christians. So I'll close this story with the way I began: What would *you* do?

■ ■ ■

It had only been a few months since a group of judges had plotted the death of their leader, Jesus Christ. Now Peter and John were standing before Annas, the high priest, and the other members of the Sanhedrin, being told what they could and could not say. The Sanhedrin meant business. This wasn't a gathering of rogue deacons who enjoyed contentious business meetings; they were the supreme court in Judea under Roman occupation.

The Sanhedrin, like our courts, had full authority to arrest individuals and rule on criminal cases. They also had the power to punish those they convicted. Their only limitation was that to carry out a death sentence, they had to have the decision ratified by the Roman procurator. In other words, the threats the disciples were facing were real.

Now keep in mind that Peter was the same disciple who, when questioned after Jesus's arrest by three different individuals, two of them young girls, about his relationship to Jesus, denied having anything to do with Him (Matthew 26:69–75). Now, this same Peter is pointing his finger straight at this powerful group of men and saying, "You are responsible for crucifying Jesus, whom God raised from the dead!"

Wow, where did that boldness come from? Short answer: *prayer!* This type of boldness to stand in the face of such hostility only comes from God. I'll talk more about how in a moment.

It was clear the Sanhedrin did not want to debate the merits of following Jesus and whether or not He was raised from the dead as Peter claimed. And for good reason! There were over five hundred people, many of them within earshot of the court, who had seen the resurrected Jesus (1 Corinthians 15:3–8). The facts were on the side of the disciples. The judges just wanted the issue to go away.

Their plan? Scare them into silence. "Let us severely threaten them, that from now on they speak to no man in this name" (Acts 4:17). Sound familiar? Here Peter, John, and the other disciples are confronted with the same threat that Angela and many like her are facing. "Don't mention the name of Jesus, or else!"

Let's face it, Jesus is the issue! Mentioning God, or religion, or spirituality is not offensive and generally raises no objections, because those terms are malleable; they do not make the exclusivity claims that come with the name Jesus. Jesus said, "I am the way, the truth, and the life. No one comes to the Father except through Me" (John 14:6).

Notice that this claim is not made by Jesus's followers about Him; this is what He stated about Himself. There are not *many* paths to a relationship with the God who created us; there is but one, and it is through His Son, Jesus Christ. If we are to truly follow Jesus Christ, we can't be silent about the fact that He is the *way*.

There are not *many* paths to a relationship with the God who created us; there is but one: Jesus Christ.

Some might say that we live in a pluralistic society and we need to be sensitive to those around us who do not share our biblical views. You are right. We need to be sensitive— sensitive to their need for a relationship with Jesus Christ!

Angela knew what God had done in her life. This courageous decision to stand for Jesus and face being thrown in jail was not something that arose from nowhere; it was a decision that had been made a hundred times before when she made the choice to trust and obey God. And each time she obeyed and trusted God, she saw Him at work in her life, giving her more of a story to tell. Just like Peter and John.

How did Peter and John respond when they were told not to speak or teach in the name of Jesus? "Which is right in God's eyes: to listen to you, or to him? You be the judges! As for us, we cannot help speaking about what we have seen and heard" (Acts 4:19–20, NIV).

MAKING IT REAL

1. What is your story? What has God done in your life? If you know Jesus and you are following Him, He is at work in your life, and like Peter, John, and Angela Hildenbrand,

you have a story. You are being called to speak about the things you have seen and heard.

2. Have you allowed fear to silence you when it comes to talking about Jesus and what He has done for you? It doesn't have to be a fear of getting in trouble with a judge or even a teacher; it may be a fear of being made fun of, of being bullied or mocked. If you have silenced yourself out of fear of what people may say or do, you have in effect denied Jesus (Matthew 10:32–33). The good news is you can make it right by asking Jesus to forgive you, and if you do, you have the confidence of knowing that He will forgive you (1 John 1:9).

3. Do you need boldness to stand up for Jesus? Do you want the kind of boldness that Peter, John, and countless others have had? Then ask for it. Make Acts 4:29–30 (next page) your prayer:

Now, Lord, look on their threats, and grant to Your servants that with all boldness they may speak Your word, by stretching out Your hand to heal, and that signs and wonders may be done through the name of Your holy Servant Jesus.

It's your turn to pray!

It's Not a Piece of Cake

It was like any other day at Melissa and Aaron Klein's business, Sweet Cakes by Melissa. Aaron, who handled the baking duties, was manning the counter so that Melissa could run some errands. Sumptuous cakes and other delights like the banana-split pizza, pecan squares, and red-velvet cookies beckoned from the display case as customers wandered in to take a look, then walked out with bags full of goodies. Few things made Aaron happier than seeing customers smile at his wife's artistry. Where other artists might use paint and canvas, Melissa "paints" with flour, shortening, eggs, and frosting, creating works of art that can only be described as irresistible.

As Aaron bent over to restock the popular pumpkin bars, a middle-aged woman walked in accompanied by a younger woman.

Like I said, it was like any other day in the bakery, but it was one that neither Aaron nor Melissa would ever forget. To understand why, I need to go back to the beginning.

Aaron was one of those guys who grew up in a Christian home but pretty much decided to live for himself instead of God. Church just wasn't for him.

"My mom made sure I was in church every Sunday, and when I was about seven years old I actually read through the entire Bible," Aaron told me. "But by the time I hit my teenage years, I knew what I wanted to do, and it wasn't church. I guess you could say I was a big party guy—loved hanging out and drinking with my buddies."

Melissa, on the other hand, seldom went to church as a young girl and knew little about the Bible.

Melissa and Aaron attended high school together—Aaron was a few grades ahead of her. They fell in love, and it turned out to be more than your typical high-school romance. Before Melissa even graduated, Aaron proposed to her and they married. She was seventeen and he was eighteen.

"Even though I wasn't a Christian, marriage was a big deal to me," Aaron explained. "Melissa wanted to move in with me until we got married, but I just didn't think it was right. And as we talked more about getting married, I made it clear to her that divorce wasn't in my vocabulary. To me, marriage was for life."

They got married, and the first few years were pretty rough. Like all couples, the newlyweds had their spats, as Melissa calls them, but they increased in frequency and intensity. Then there was Aaron's partying. Melissa thought it was getting out of hand, driving a wedge between them. And it was during this time that she began to hunger for God.

Aaron's grandparents were strong Christians, and Melissa was drawn to them. With the exception of her maternal grandmother, Melissa never knew her grandparents. But it was more than just the typical laidback ways of a grandma and grandpa. Aaron's grandparents had something, a peace, a way of making life work that attracted Melissa. Melissa eventually discovered what the secret ingredient was when she accepted Jesus Christ as her personal Savior. But her newfound inner peace only seemed to create more external tension between her and Aaron.

Even though I wasn't a Christian, marriage was a big deal to me.

"I decided to confront Aaron with his partying one last time, but what I didn't know was that God was already working on him. We were sitting on our front porch, and I told him the partying needed to stop and that we needed to start getting involved in church and doing the right things."

Aaron was more than ready.

"I was the prodigal, and knew it was time to turn my life over to the Lord," he explained. "And then we just started getting heavily involved in church, working with the youth group, and making God number one in our lives."

Shortly after they surrendered to Christ, God blessed them with an opportunity that neither of them ever thought was possible.

"I always loved baking cakes, but when our first child's first birthday approached, I went all out. I created a two-tiered cake with airplanes and race cars and clouds on it. I guess the guests liked what I did because it wasn't long before friends and family began asking me to bake their kids' birthday cakes. When they started offering to pay for my cakes, I began thinking about opening my own little bakery."

Thinking about owning your own business and actually following through are two different things. At the time, Aaron was driving a truck while Melissa stayed home with their son. Raising capital to start a business was out of the question. At least in human terms.

"The only way to describe how we started our business is to say God gave it to us," Aaron offered.

With no capital and not even having to dip into their personal savings, they opened Sweet Cakes by Melissa.

"We decided from day one that we would honor God in the way we ran our business," Aaron told me. "We put Bible verses on our website and hung inspirational messages on the walls of our bakery. Played Christian music. Before we opened, we asked our pastor to come and dedicate the business to God. Not once did anyone object to our expressions of faith; in fact, people often said they appreciated our openness about our faith."

Until that day when Aaron was tending the counter and the woman and her daughter came into the store. They were there for a cake tasting for a wedding. Aaron didn't recognize the mother, but she had been a previous customer. In fact she had told Melissa at a recent bridal show how much she loved her own wedding cake from Sweet Cakes.

"She was all excited, but as she talked about the upcoming wedding, it became clear to me that her daughter was marrying another woman."

Aaron knew what he had to do.

"As I said earlier, marriage is a big deal to me, and because I believe the Bible, marriage is a sacred union between a man and a woman."

He politely explained to the woman that because of his faith in Jesus and obedience to the Bible he could not in good conscience create a cake that would celebrate something he did not believe in.

According to Aaron, the woman seemed a little disappointed, but she left without comment. He headed back into the kitchen to grab some cupcakes for the display case, thinking little about what had just happened. But as he walked back into the store, the door opened, and that's when the fireworks began.

"She was clearly upset and started accusing me of hypocrisy and discrimination and a few other things," Aaron recalled. "I mean, it was pretty intense. She even tried to goad me into a theological debate, telling me that Christians are supposed to love everyone and not judge others. I let her have her say, and my only response to her was to tell her I believed what the Bible says. After she had her say, she left, and once again, I thought that was the end of it."

We decided from day one that we would honor God in the way we ran our business.

It wasn't. About ten days after the incident, Aaron and Melissa were notified by the US Department of Justice that they were being investigated for discrimination. Aaron could hardly believe what was happening, so he e-mailed the *Lars Larson Show.* The radio show e-mailed back, asking him to come on the show. Before he knew it, he was on the air explaining what happened. Within half an hour, there was an influx of customers.

"The next day, more than two hundred new customers showed up wanting to buy stuff," Aaron laughed. "Then the next day we had a line outside our shop that stretched for a block and a half. We couldn't bake enough product to keep up with the demand."

That's when the opposition raised the stakes with what can only be called bullying. This is typical behavior by those who believe in freedom of speech for everyone but followers of Christ.

The Kleins began receiving threatening e-mails and voice-mail messages, calling them names like "racist maggots" and telling them to "do everyone a favor and fall off a cliff." Most of the messages they received would be inappropriate to include here. It's sadly ironic—and quite common—for people to use hate speech when accusing Christians of hatred. But the attacks didn't stop there. Activists began targeting vendors who did business with Sweet Cakes by Melissa, and within days almost all of those vendors canceled their accounts with the Kleins.

"That was one of the lowest points for me," Melissa admitted. "We had worked so hard to build our business, and those customers were our friends as well. One of those customers was responsible for 50 percent of our business, so this was really hard for me."

Eventually the Department of Justice dropped the investigation, but Oregon's Bureau of Labor and Industry took up the cause, claiming that Aaron and Melissa were guilty of violating Oregon's law prohibiting discrimination based on sexual preference. But according to Aaron, that wasn't why he refused to sell a wedding cake to the lesbian couple.

"We believe God loves everyone, and we try to as well," he explained. "We've sold birthday cakes to homosexuals and probably a lot of other people whose lifestyles we disagree with. But we draw the line at marriage. We once had someone come in and wanted us to design a cake celebrating her divorce, but we refused. Marriage to us is sacred, and we just couldn't celebrate a marriage that did not conform to God's design."

Unfortunately, the Bureau of Labor and Industry thought otherwise, slapping up to $150,000 in damages on the couple. Although their church and other organizations had been raising money to help support them, Melissa and Aaron were forced to close their business. They currently run a scaled-down version of Sweet Cakes by Melissa out of their home and have no regrets about the stand they took.

"Hey, I used to be a mechanic and a garbage man," Aaron laughed. "We dedicated our business to God, and He allowed it to prosper for a season. He's taken care of us through all of this turmoil, and I know He'll take care of us in the future."

Still, Aaron admits to moments of discouragement. "What was really difficult for me was to have people who identified themselves as Christians attack us for our stand, especially when they twisted the Bible to say what they wanted it to say."

Both Melissa and Aaron miss their bakery, but given the chance to do a replay, they wouldn't change a thing.

> Marriage to us is sacred, and we just couldn't celebrate a marriage that did not conform to God's design.

"I've searched my heart over and over," Melissa confessed. "I asked God to show me if I was wrong. I searched the Scriptures and sought counsel from our pastor. If the stand we took was wrong, I wanted to apologize, make it right. I'm not really a confrontational person, so this was really difficult for me. But the Bible is so clear in its teaching on marriage that we just had to obey God rather than man."

Increasingly, Christians who own businesses will face similar attacks. The Enemy knows that it's a lot harder to stand up for what you believe when your income is at stake. So what would Aaron say to other Christians in business who may feel pressured to abandon their convictions?

"You can trust the Lord. You can rely completely on Him.

Jesus told us that if He takes such good care of the birds and the flowers, how much more will He take care of us, and we found that to be true. When we couldn't pay our electric bill, our church paid it for us. Had I done the wrong thing, the world would have been happy with me. But by doing the right thing, I was able to experience the support of other Christians. God honored me for my stand, and He will do the same for anyone who obeys Him."

■ ■ ■

> By faith Noah, being divinely warned of things not yet
> seen, moved with godly fear. (Hebrews 11:7)

Everyone has fears. The question is not, do you have fears? The question is, do your fears have you?

Aaron and Melissa certainly had fears, but those fears, which are rooted in a fear of man, were eclipsed by a fear of or reverence for God. Noah provides a great example of how a fear of God overcomes the fear of man.

To say that Noah lived in a morally and spiritually challenging environment would be an understatement. Genesis 6 says that God looked upon the earth and saw that it was so corrupt and violent that He said He was actually sorry He had made man in the first place.

By the way, Jesus said in Matthew 24 that the moral and cultural conditions of the earth at the time of His return would be like the days of Noah before the Flood. So this would suggest that Noah is also a timely and relevant example for us.

God told Noah that judgment was coming. He was going to

destroy the inhabitants of the earth because of the sinfulness of man, so He told Noah to build an ark through which He would save the human race and the animal kingdom.

This was not a call to take up a new hobby that Noah could hide in his backyard or in the garage. This was a mammoth building project that is estimated to have been at least four hundred fifty feet long, seventy-five feet wide, and forty-five feet high. It took between fifty and seventy-five years to build.

> **This was not a call to take up a new hobby that Noah could hide in his backyard or in the garage.**

Consider for a moment the commitment Noah was making when he said yes to God. This was not a weekend project; this was an investment of a large portion of his energy, his resources, his entire life. This was a decision that would forever define Noah.

So it is with us when we are prompted by the Holy Spirit to accept Jesus as our Savior and commit our lives to following Him. It is not a weekend-only obligation; it is an all-consuming decision to put the purposes and plans of God at the center of our lives, and that includes our occupations. Melissa and Aaron Klein certainly have learned this!

Now keep in mind that while Noah was building this huge houseboat on dry land, preparing for the coming flood, the idea of a flood was a foreign concept. While we don't know for certain, there is scriptural support to suggest that the earth had not experienced rain prior to the Flood (Genesis 2:5–6), which of course only added to the peculiarity of Noah and his project.

During the half a century or more that it took Noah to build the ark, he was raising his family and preaching righteousness

(2 Peter 2:5) to a society that in every way had rejected God and His truth. God did not call Noah to some secret society; rather He wanted Noah to be public and to warn the people of the pending destruction of the earth. He wanted Noah by both example and word to challenge the culture.

Imagine the fear that Noah had of being ridiculed, rejected, and persecuted by a society that had turned its back on God and His truths. Today Noah would have been called an extremist, out of touch with reality, a fearmonger, a hater; and they would have probably called him hydrophobic. Late-night comedians would have flooded the airwaves with their jokes designed to mock and marginalize Noah and anyone who would dare to associate with him.

Noah had a greater reverence *for* God than he had a fear *of* men.

The Bible says that "Noah did according to all that LORD commanded him" (Genesis 7:5). According to Hebrews 11:7, rather than be paralyzed by the fear of what men would say and do to him, Moses *moved* with fear of God. This is not suggesting that Noah was caught in between a fear of the godless culture and a fear of God, trying to decide which one presented a greater threat to him.

The fear Noah had of God is better understood as a reverence or awe *for* God. In other words, Noah had a greater reverence *for* God than he had a fear *of* men. It was this reverence for God and a desire to obey Him that enabled Noah to overcome the very real and tangible fears that come with being the only one standing for God.

Fortunately, no matter what your predicament is, it is not going to be as bad as Noah's. While it may appear that you are alone in your stand for Jesus and the truth of God's Word, there are still many who have not bowed their knee to the god of this age (Romans 11:3–5)—you are not alone!

MAKING IT REAL

1. Noah's life was marked by his commitment to obey God. Those around Noah had no questions about where Noah stood. They didn't agree with him, but they knew he stood with God and His truth. If you have made a commitment to follow Jesus, is it of such priority to you that you are marked and your family and friends see it?

2. Is your fear of or reverence for God such that it trumps the fears you have of what others might say or do because you openly embrace Jesus and the truth of God's Word?

3. God may not be telling you to build an ark in your back-yard, but what is He telling you to do that, like Noah, will define you as a follower of Jesus?

12

"God Is Good! All the Time!"

It would have been so easy. Just say the words and all the suffering would end. The iron shackles and chains would come off. Instead of the dank, cold floor, she could be resting in the comfort of her home. The child she was carrying in her belly would be born in a hospital, not a prison. But she had better say them soon. Time was running out. The sentence of death loomed over her head. But she could escape it. There was a way out. Just say the words.

"I renounce my faith in Jesus Christ."

I wrestled with including Mariam Ibraheem's story in this book. For one thing, I was one of many people directly involved in lobbying for her release, and I didn't want it to appear that I was promoting either myself or the Family Research Council, the organization I lead. Also, most of us can relate to the other stories in this book, but this one? Its setting is Sudan, a nation unfamiliar to most of us. Mariam speaks no English, making it difficult to interview her—I would have to rely on secondhand sources along with my limited personal interaction with her. And then there's the consequence she faced for taking a stand. Not to minimize the costs everyone else in this book faced for staying true to their beliefs—ridicule, loss of opportunity, maybe a fine or brief jail sentence—but the stakes for Mariam exceeded anything any of us will ever face.

Death.

Which is why I decided to include her story. I'm sure most Christians believe that if it ever came to the ultimate price to pay for belief in Jesus, we would not hesitate to sacrifice our lives. Or at least we like to think we would. Would *you* take a stand for Christ if it meant certain death? Would *I*? For most of us, that's a hypothetical question. For Mariam, martyrdom was not an intellectual concept to discuss in the comfort of a small group or Bible study. It's what she faced if she did not turn her back on Jesus.

So I've decided to close with Mariam's story in hopes that it will inspire and encourage you (give you courage) to stand boldly for Jesus. Almost every day we have opportunities to publicly acknowledge our faith in Jesus, yet just as Peter did, we shrink into silence. We don't want to offend anyone, or we don't want to seem foolish. Mariam cared only about one thing: remaining true to her Savior. Here's how it happened.

Mariam was born in Western Sudan to a Muslim father and a Christian mother. When she was six, her father left the family, and Mariam was raised as a Christian. As a young girl, Mariam demonstrated a flair for business, eventually opening a successful hair salon and a small convenience store inside of a shopping center. She also held an interest in agricultural land.

In 2011, when she was twenty-four years old, Mariam fell in love with Daniel Wani, a Christian from South Sudan who was also an American citizen. They married later that year, and that's where Mariam's troubles began. Apparently, one of Mariam's relatives contacted authorities, accusing her of committing adultery. According to Islamic law, a Muslim woman cannot marry a non-Muslim man. So by marrying Daniel, a Christian, her marriage was not recognized, and she was therefore committing adultery by living with a man who was not her husband. In May 2014, twenty-seven-year-old Mariam stood before a judge who "kindly" offered to drop all charges if she would abandon her Christian faith and convert to Islam.

> I am a Christian, and I will remain a Christian, she boldly declared before the judge.

Imagine being a successful young woman, happily married and facing such a serious charge. By now, Mariam and Daniel had welcomed their first child, Martin, into their lives, and Mariam was pregnant with their second child. All she had to do was nod in agreement to the judge's offer and everything would return to normal. Except to Mariam, faith in Jesus was not negotiable.

"The situation was difficult…. I was given three days [to convert to Islam]…. While I was in prison, some people came to visit me from the Muslim Scholars Association. These were Imams that created an intervention by citing parts of the Quran for me. I faced a tremendous amount of pressure," she later explained to Fox News anchor Megyn Kelly. Most of the other national media ignored Mariam's plight. In my opinion, if it wasn't for Megyn and Fox, this alarming account of religious persecution would never have been heard by the world.

Mariam refused to renounce her Christian faith.

"I am a Christian, and I will remain a Christian," she boldly declared before the judge.

The charges were serious: adultery and converting to Christianity. For adultery, she would receive one hundred lashes, but for converting to Christianity, the sentence handed down by the judge was death by hanging. Again, the judge showed his "mercy." The lashing and hanging would be postponed until she gave birth. Yet the entire time she was in prison awaiting her execution, Mariam was shackled to the wall with heavy iron chains and handcuffs. At one point during her imprisonment, Daniel was allowed to visit her and was shocked to see the way her legs and arms were swollen from the shackles. Even when she eventually gave birth to her baby daughter in a filthy prison cell, Mariam was chained to a hospital bed brought in for the delivery.

"The situation was difficult, but I was sure that God would stand by my side. I relied only on my faith," she later told Kelly.

Because Daniel was an American citizen, he thought his government would intervene. After all, the United States has historically been a champion of liberty around the world. His pleas for help, however, fell on deaf ears. The United States embassy in Sudan refused to assist Mariam, even insulting the young family by requesting DNA to prove that Daniel was indeed the father of Martin, their child who was imprisoned with Mariam. And the State Department did its best to dodge the issue until pressured by faith-based organizations, sympathetic politicians, and ordinary Christians. In fairness to the current administration, over the years I have witnessed both Republican and Democratic administrations do their best to avoid getting involved in cases where Christians were being persecuted in Muslim nations.

Maybe that's a good thing, because it forces us to rely on a more powerful and reliable resource.

"I am just praying to God," Daniel sighed after yet another snub from his government. "He can do a miracle."

Throughout this entire ordeal, more than forty organizations—most of them faith based—used their influence to try and free Mariam. We were joined by a number of members of Congress—notably Senator Ted Cruz, as well as congressmen Chris Smith, Mark Meadows, Frank Wolf, and Trent Franks. But more important, Christians all over the world began praying for her release. I've not been one who engages in public protest much, but we teamed up with religious-liberty organizations for a rally in front of the White House to call attention to Mariam's plight. Additionally, more than fifty thousand people signed a petition on the White House website, urging the president to take action on Mariam's behalf. There were dozens of meetings and phone calls with senators, congressmen, and even Maowia Khalid, the Sudanese ambassador to the United States.

Apparently, all the public attention to Mariam's cause was working. After nearly six months of lobbying for her release, we got word that the charges had been dropped and that Mariam would soon be free. In an appeals hearing, the judge reversed her sentence and ordered her release. Around the globe, Christians cheered the news. Mariam's attorney, Elshareef Mohammed, heard the report on the radio and rushed to the court to make sure it was true. And while this was welcome news, many of us knew that Mariam's life might be more endangered as a Christian woman outside the prison than in. The public's interest in Mariam's case had forced the US State Department to engage more aggressively, and as a result, upon release she and her two young children were taken to a safe house while her travel documents were put in order.

After a short delay, Mariam and her family were on their way to the airport to board a plane for America. But when they got to the airport, Sudanese authorities detained them, claiming they were trying to leave the country illegally. Shortly after learning of this last-minute attempt to keep Mariam in a country where she clearly could be targeted for her faith, I again spoke with Ambassador Khalid and emphasized to him the concerns that millions of Christians in the United States had regarding this latest development with Mariam and her family. He assured me that Mariam and her family were safe, and that his government was working to process the necessary paperwork allowing them to leave. I wanted to believe him, but the events surrounding Mariam's imprisonment had eroded my confidence in anything that the Sudanese government—or even our government—could do. Clearly Mariam's fate rested in God's hands.

I'll never forget the phone call I got one Thursday night in July from Congressman Mark Meadows. Just hours after I testified on behalf of Mariam on Capitol Hill before the House Foreign Affairs Subcommittee, word came she was safe.

"Mariam and her children are on a plane. They've left Sudan!"

This brave young mother—only twenty-seven years old— could have avoided this whole frightening ordeal by simply saying a few words—even if she didn't really mean them. She could have crossed her fingers behind her back and renounced her faith in Jesus. But she stood strong, knowing that she would be thrown in prison with her toddler son, give birth in that prison, and then be hanged. Where does that courage come from?

Three months after Mariam's release, the organization I lead honored her at our annual Values Voter Summit. After we made her our first-ever recipient of the Cost of Discipleship Award, Mariam addressed the crowd who had gathered at the Omni Shoreham Hotel in Washington, DC.

In her limited English, she stood before the overflowing ballroom and said, "God is good! All the time! God is good. You must believe in the Lord and follow Him in all your steps because He loves us all."

After thanking those who helped secure her release and paying tribute to her husband, Daniel, she closed by directing our attention to a couple in Iran in the dangerous throes of religious persecution.

Through an interpreter she said, "I would like to greet my sister, Naghmeh, the wife of the fighter Pastor Abedini. Tell her do not fear, be strong, take care of your kids, and the Lord will be with you. God is good! God is good!"

In her new language of English, she stood before the overflowing ballroom and said, "God is good! All the time!"

I do not want to minimize the courage it takes for Americans to take a stand for their faith. If you try to openly live out your faith, you will be ridiculed, ostracized, and bullied. Your beliefs could even get you fired. Many Christians resign themselves to "flying under the radar," or as the song we used to sing says, "hide it under a bushel." You may never be asked to renounce your faith in order to spare your life, but the pressure to keep your faith to yourself has never been greater and will only increase. And that is why I decided to share Mariam's story. Whenever you are tempted to cave in and let the world squeeze you into its mold, take courage from these words of Mariam's: "Do not fear. God is good!"

■ ■ ■

But you shall receive power when the Holy Spirit has come upon you; and you shall be witnesses to Me in Jerusalem, and in all Judea and Samaria, and to the end of the earth. (Acts 1:8)

Would you be willing to die for your faith? Most of us would say yes. Some might go so far as to even respond like Peter did to Jesus, when Jesus warned His disciples that they would all soon distance themselves from Him. "Even if I have to die with You, I will not deny You!" (Matthew 26:35).

Would you be willing to die for your faith?

You know the rest of the story: Peter did not deny Jesus just once; he denied Him three times! I don't think Peter was blowing smoke. I think his intentions were genuine, but something was missing in his moment of testing. After Jesus's resurrection, Peter was forgiven and reconciled to his friend and now Savior. Just prior to Jesus ascending into heaven, He commissioned Peter and the other disciples, giving them the authority to carry out the tasks of making the truth known to men, women, and children, introducing them to Jesus, and teaching them to follow Him.

But Jesus told them to first wait in Jerusalem to receive the power needed to fulfill this commission (Acts 1:1–11). That promised power was the Holy Spirit. "But you shall receive power when the Holy Spirit has come upon you; and you shall be witnesses to Me in Jerusalem, and in all Judea and Samaria, and to the end of the earth" (verse 8).

As Peter discovered, the best intentions, even the truest devotion, are not enough when the threats and attacks move from the theoretical to the real and tangible. What transformed Peter from a coward to a gospel crusader? Boldness. And that only comes through the power of the Holy Spirit.

I understand there are differing views among Bible-believing Christians on the workings of the Holy Spirit, but don't worry, I won't get all theological on you. Instead, I want us to focus on how the Holy Spirit influences the way we live.

Paul told the believers living in Ephesus, a culture that was very similar to our own, "Do not be drunk with wine, in which is dissipation [waste]; but be filled with the Spirit" (Ephesians 5:18). Scripture teaches that everyone who has trusted Jesus Christ as their Savior and Lord also receives the Holy Spirit, by whom they are sealed (Ephesians 1:13). If all believers have the Holy Spirit, why would Paul say we need to be filled with the Holy Spirit, comparing this filling to wine?

Just because we have the Holy Spirit does not mean we allow ourselves to be influenced and controlled by Him. Whether you recognize it or not, you are going to live under the influence of something. Paul says let it be the Holy Spirit.

How do we live under the influence of the Holy Spirit so that we can have the boldness of Peter, Mariam, and others in this book, as well as those throughout the history of Christendom who have stood resolutely for Jesus in the face of death itself?

First, we need to realize that we can't live under the influence of the Holy Spirit by only going to church on Sunday, filling up our "Holy Spirit tank," and then driving off on a moral and spiritual detour for the rest of the week. Living under the influence of the Holy Spirit is not a part-time, weekend activity.

Whether you recognize it or not, you are going to live under the influence of something.

Living under the influence of the Holy Spirit is a full-time daily undertaking. We choose whether or not we will live under the influence of the Holy Spirit by what we listen to, what we watch, what we think about, and what we do. In Romans 12:1–2, Paul gives us an illustration of what living under the influence of the Holy Spirit looks like: "I beseech you therefore, brethren, by the mercies of God, that you present your bodies a living sacrifice, holy, acceptable to God, which is your reasonable service. And do not be conformed to this world, but be transformed by the renewing of your mind, that you may prove what is that good and acceptable and perfect will of God."

Notice where Paul starts? It's not just our minds and emotions that are to be yielded to God, but our bodies as well. Paul challenges us to present our bodies as "living sacrifices," which communicates the all-consuming nature of this call. The Jewish reader and those Gentiles of that day familiar with Jewish ceremonial law understood that a sacrificial animal had to be without spot or blemish (Leviticus 1:3). Not just any old sacrifice would do; it had to be holy and acceptable.

Likewise, you and I are to present our bodies holy and acceptable. This doesn't mean we are perfect and free from sin, but it does mean that we will not willfully and repeatedly engage in behavior that God says is wrong (1 Corinthians 6:9–10; Galatians 5:19–21). Paul also says this is our reasonable service. In other words, this is not for extra credit; this is what is expected of each of us.

You may be wondering how you can ever hope to accomplish such a significant challenge of being holy and living by God's standards when it seems everyone and everything around you is essentially telling you to forget God and His outdated standards. Paul has the answer: "And do not be conformed to this world, but be transformed by the renewing of your mind" (Romans 12:2). In other words, do not live according to the style or manner of this present age but through renewing your mind. How do you do that? Good question. It is through what we look at. Job said he made a covenant with his eyes not to look at that which would tempt him to think lustful thoughts (Job 31:1). Jesus said, "If your right eye causes you to sin, pluck it out" (Matthew 5:29).

Jesus wasn't saying we should start literally pulling our eyes out, but that we need to take drastic actions to keep from looking at that which would cause us to sin. For instance, if you have a problem with pornography on the Internet, get rid of your computer. Does the music you listen to prompt thoughts that are dishonoring to God? Time to get rid of the music! I know that sounds drastic in the twenty-first century, but that's what Jesus is saying. Get away from anything that causes you to sin, but then replace those things with something better: things that are true, honorable, right, pure, and gracious (Philippians 4:8). What we think about directs how we act.

Having the boldness to stand for Jesus in the face of death begins with choosing to be under the influence of the Holy Spirit each and every day.

MAKING IT REAL

1. Put yourself in the situation Mariam Ibraheem was in. Would you be willing to die for your faith in Jesus Christ?

2. Being that the possibility of execution for our faith in Christ is almost nonexistent for us living in the United States, it is fairly easy for us to say we would be willing to die. Let me put the question another way. Are you willing to live according to your faith in Jesus Christ?

3. Write down three steps you can take to start coming under the influence of the Holy Spirit each day.

13

Writing the Next Chapter

By no means am I a movie buff, but if you were to ask my wife or kids for a list of my favorite movies, they would most likely rattle off about five or six movies that I've seen enough times to recite many of the lines. One of those movies is *Twelve O'Clock High* starring Gregory Peck as General Frank Savage.

In this age of high definition and surround sound, you've probably not seen this black-and-white motion picture. While the sensory experience may fall far short of your idea of a movie, it is still worth watching. Released in 1949, the movie depicts the army's Eighth Air Force that flew daylight precision bombing raids against Nazi Germany in WWII.

The daring daylight raids were dangerous. The high number of B-17s shot down and the crew members killed or missing in action was having a physiological effect upon the remaining men as they feared they would be next. This fear of death combined with a pronounced lack of discipline within the squadron had put morale into a tailspin. The fictional commander, Colonel Keith Davenport, was relieved of duty, and Brigadier General Frank Savage was then placed in command.

Upon assuming command Savage assembles the men and says, "We've got to fight. And some of us have got to die. I'm not trying to tell you not to be afraid. Fear is normal. But stop worrying about it and about yourselves. Stop making plans. Forget about going home. Consider yourselves already dead. Once you accept that idea, it won't be so tough." With that he walked out of the room.

Sounds pretty harsh! But isn't that what Jesus essentially told His disciples when He said, "If anyone desires to come after Me, let him deny himself, and take up his cross, and follow Me" (Matthew 16:24)? There was no reason to take up a cross, an instrument of execution, unless it was for the purpose of dying. Jesus was saying, "If you want to follow Me, stop worrying about yourselves. Stop making plans. Consider yourselves already dead." Once we come to the point where our lives do not matter, we are ready to follow Jesus and be used by Him.

There is a reason Jesus tells us to basically consider ourselves already dead. Fear of death is common, and it keeps us from living life to its fullest. As Sir William Wallace, a leader of the Wars of Scottish Independence, was quoted as saying, "Every man dies. Not every man really lives." In other words, many people are so afraid of dying, they never live!

Jesus came to free us from the fear of death and the fear of life. The reason death is such a common fear is the uncertainty many have about what awaits beyond the grave. Let me ask you, are you afraid of death? I know that is not a question you normally ask someone, but if you truly want to live a life of *no fear,* it begins with overcoming the fear of death.

Let's be clear; I am not talking about being someone who

glorifies death or is preoccupied with the darkness of death. Such a fixation with death is often an overcompensation stemming from the fear they have of death. What I am talking about is making peace with God and settling the question of where you will spend eternity.

It is not easy, but it is simple.

You and I are born separated from God because of sin. And unless we are reconciled to God, we will die separated from Him and spend eternity in a place the Bible calls

> **Jesus came to free us from the fear of death and the fear of life.**

hell. Jesus describes hell as a place of perpetual torment where people will forever be separated from God. That is reason enough to fear death.

Here is the good news: we don't have to stay separated from God. In fact, Jesus Christ came to this earth, lived a sinless life, died on the cross to pay the penalty for my sins and for your sins, and was then raised from the dead so that we would no longer be separated from God. God actually wants to have a relationship with you, which is why He sent Jesus.

Here is all that is required of you to experience a relationship with the God who created you: "If you confess with your mouth the Lord Jesus and believe in your heart that God has raised Him from the dead, you will be saved" (Romans 10:9).

If you don't have that relationship but would like to, just ask God to help you know Him. You might say something like this: "God, I know that I am separated from You because of sin, my sin. Please forgive me of all my sin. I believe that Jesus is Your Son. That He died on the cross for my sin. That He was buried and then rose to life again. I accept Jesus as my Savior, and today

I make Him the Lord of my life. From this day forward I want to live for You. No longer will I fear man, but I will reverence You in all that I do. Thank You for saving me!"

Jesus said that He came to the earth that we may have life, and have it more abundantly (John 10:10). The reality is, we are not ready to truly live until we are ready to die. Once you have accepted Jesus Christ as your Lord and Savior, you not only have *eternal* life, you have freedom from fear so that you can live the *abundant* life—a life filled with meaning and purpose.

So, consider yourself already dead—that you might truly live . . . and go write the next chapter of *No Fear*!

Acknowledgments

For me, communicating from behind a microphone on radio or television actually comes much more naturally than sitting down at a keyboard and writing a book. That might partially explain why this book, from the original concept to completion, was a four-and-a-half-year project.

As with any worthwhile project that I have been a part of, *No Fear* was a team effort from start to finish.

You would not be holding this book in your hands had my friend Robert Wolgemuth not repeatedly encouraged me to take on this project. Robert and his associate Austin Wilson helped guide me through each step of the process, connecting me with some great people that not only helped make *No Fear* a reality; they actually made it enjoyable!

First in that category is Lyn Cryderman, whose skill at the keyboard enabled me to spend a little more time behind the microphone. Lyn, you're a true professional.

Then there is Bruce Nygren and the team at WaterBrook who have been a delight to work with. Thanks for putting on the polish!

From my personal team I want to thank Randy Burt, who helped facilitate the hours of recorded interviews that went into telling the stories of *No Fear*. Without the help of my executive assistant, Lindsay Hoefer, who helped coordinate every aspect of

No Fear with her trademark of excellence, it would have probably never crossed the finish line.

I want to say thank you to Richard Perkins, for providing the preface and for being my dad!

Finally and most importantly, I want to thank my wife, Lawana, and my five blessings from the Lord—Kendal, Rachel, David, Grace, and Samuel—for taking care of the many projects around the house while I was working on *No Fear*. I also appreciate your attempts to not disturb me, in those rare moments of inspiration, by tiptoeing past my study in an effort to keep the wood floors from creaking. I knew you were there—and was thankful for it!

About the Author

Tony Perkins is Family Research Council's fourth and longest-serving president, joining the organization in August of 2003. Described as a legislative pioneer by the national media, he has established himself as an innovative pro-life and pro-family policy and political leader since first being elected to office in 1996.

Keeping his commitment to serving only two terms, Tony had a significant impact on politics in his home state of Louisiana as a state representative and as a candidate for the United States Senate in 2002. He was a tireless advocate for the family during his tenure in the Louisiana State Legislature, where he authored and passed the nation's first Covenant Marriage law in 1997.

Tony is an ordained minister who is active in Christian ministries, serving as an elder in his home church and frequently speaking at other churches across the country. He is the host of a daily syndicated radio show, *Washington Watch,* and he frequently appears as a guest on national news programs and talk shows. A veteran of the United States Marine Corps and a former police officer, Tony holds a bachelor of science from Liberty University and a master of public administration from Louisiana State University. He also has an honorary doctorate of divinity from Liberty University. He and his wife, Lawana, have been married since 1986 and have five children.